Latinas in LAW ENFORCEMENT

Stories of Leading with Courage and Breaking
Boundaries Beyond the Badge

MICHELLE J. VELASQUEZ
ESMERALDA SAMANIEGO

Latinas in
LAW ENFORCEMENT

For more information visit:
Fig Factor Media | www.figfactormedia.com
Latinas in Law Enforcement | www.latinasinlawenforcement.com

Cover Design by DG Marco Alvarez
Layout by LDG Juan Manuel Serna Rosales

Printed in the United States of America

FIG
FACTOR
MEDIA

ISBN: 978-1-961600-52-2
Library of Congress Number: 2025907294

This book is dedicated to all the Latinas in law enforcement—past, present, and future—who serve with unwavering dedication, courage, and resilience.

To the trailblazing women who came before us: Your strength shattered barriers and paved the way for future generations. Though we may never fully grasp the challenges you faced, we honor your sacrifices and stand on the foundation you built.

To our fallen sisters in blue: Your service, bravery, and ultimate sacrifice will never be forgotten. Your legacy lives on in the stories we share and the lives you touched.

To the young women and future leaders in law enforcement—our explorers, cadets, and youth program participants: May you find inspiration in these pages, knowing that your dreams are possible and your potential is limitless.

Finally, to our families, significant others, children, and friends: Thank you for your patience, support, and understanding. Your love and sacrifices make our service possible. This journey is not ours alone, it is yours as well.

TABLE OF CONTENTS

ACKNOWLEDGMENTS

First and foremost, I want to thank God for the opportunity to share my story and for keeping me safe during my law enforcement career. I am deeply grateful to my family—my dad, mom, sisters, nieces, and nephews—for their unwavering support.

To my rock, my husband, Martin Arteaga, thank you for holding down the fort at home while I dedicated myself to protecting our country. To my four amazing children—Marty, Izan, Joe, and Adaleah—thank you for sharing me with my department. I want you to know that every day I gave my all to bring justice and keep our communities safe. Each night, I went home knowing I had done my absolute best.

I also extend my gratitude to the dedicated employees of the US Customs and Border Protection Chicago Field Office and Area Port of Chicago for their commitment and sacrifice in safeguarding our nation. It was an honor to work alongside the incredible men and women throughout my sixteen-year career at Homeland Security Investigations (HSI), Crime Prevention and Information Center (CPIC), Federal Bureau of Investigation (FBI), US Drug Enforcement Administration (DEA), High Intensity Drug Trafficking Area (HIDTA), Illinois State Police (ISP), and Chicago Police Department (CPD). A special thank you to Deputy Assistant Director Anye Whyte for being a mentor and guiding force in my career.

Last but certainly not least, to my partner in crime, Officer Arredondo—the man who stood by my side throughout my entire career—thank you, buddy, for all you have done and continue to do. Your support, friendship, and dedication have meant the world to me.

—**Michelle J. Velasquez**

First and foremost, I want to thank God for the life He has given me, for His strength, guidance, and for blessing me with a family that has shaped me into who I am today.

To my family—my father, my mother, my brothers, and my sisters—your love and support have been my foundation. Every sacrifice you have made, every word of encouragement, and every lesson you have taught me has guided me on this journey.

To my significant other and his supportive family, thank you for believing in me and encouraging me to write this book, and for always standing by me and showing your unconditional love. Your support means the world to me.

To my nieces and nephews and my future children, you are my heart and my inspiration. I hope this book shows you that you can achieve anything with hard work, determination, and faith.

To ALL my friends, your encouragement and constant support have kept me going. I am forever grateful for your presence in my life.

To the US Customs and Border Protection Chicago Field Office, Area Port of Chicago, and the CBP Explorers—thank you for twenty-two years of growth and opportunities and the years to come. This career has shaped me in countless ways, and I am grateful for every experience and every person who has helped me along the way and will continue to guide me.

Finally, to all my mentors, thank you for your wisdom, your leadership, and your belief in my potential. Your influence has been invaluable, and I carry your lessons with me every day.

This book is not just my story, it is a tribute to all of you. Thank you for being part of my journey.

—**Esmeralda Samaniego**

FOREWORD

"We can be a character in a story written by someone else or we can choose to be the author of our own story." —**Ruby Garcia**

Everyone has a story to tell; it is best to tell that story in your own voice.

I am proud of these women who are sharing their stories in this book. Theirs are stories of service and sacrifice that otherwise would have been lost to the winds of time. These stories also will serve as a beacon during some of life's storms that young women, especially Latinas, can follow to guide them safely to shore.

I was never one of those children who said at age five or ten or even at eighteen, *"When I grow up, I want to be a..."* I had so many interests, most ideas coming from the books that transported me to other times and places. I always read a wide variety of books, everything from George Orwell to Agatha Christie and lots of biographies of famous and not-so-famous people.

Growing up in a time—the 1950s—and in a place—Chicago—with many of life's challenges, rife with poverty and racial unrest, I often got not-too-subtle messages that somehow daughters were less valuable than sons. I quickly rejected all those notions that said all I could ever aspire to be was a wife or maybe a schoolteacher. The stories of adventure that I got from books were burned into my soul, and I decided to become an adventurer, too. I wanted to travel the world, which I did. I was always more intrepid than afraid, and I wanted to try new things like learning to ride a motorcycle, or hang-gliding over the Atlantic Ocean, or skiing in the Alps, or even flying a plane, all of which I did and more.

My greatest adventure lasted nearly twenty-five years, starting when I became the first Latina Illinois state trooper in 1979. I was convinced that with the right training and a little support, I could do anything the job threw at me. Requests for training were never-ending and often rejected, but I found ways around those rejections. And hoping for support was generally nonexistent for women in those days.

Things have improved over the years. But some obstacles still remain, especially for Latina officers, who are dramatically underrepresented in law enforcement in Illinois and across the country. Illinois has a Latino population of nearly 20 percent, but fewer than 5 percent are Latina police officers. The ISP number is even lower, with just over 1 percent.

It wasn't until I discovered the camaraderie and training opportunities offered by the International Association of Women Police (IAWP), which I joined in 1981, that I knew I was going to make it. I met hundreds of women in law enforcement from around the world, they became my role models and mentors. That experience propelled me and a handful of other women to establish Illinois Women in Law Enforcement in 1985, using

IAWP as our template. But I don't think my story is unusual or exceptional. It is every woman in law enforcement's story, but it has never been told, until now!

Women supporting women, not just in law enforcement, has been important throughout my career and even in retirement. So, in 2017, in an effort to encourage more Latinas to consider a career in law enforcement, I established Latinas in Law Enforcement (LILE) in the Illinois Scholarship Fund at Elgin Community College.

I was honored when Michelle Velasquez, a facilitator for this book, asked me to write a few words expressing my viewpoint on the importance of Latinas telling their stories. The stories in this book will help shine a bright light on a profession dedicated **to serve and protect** our families, our neighborhoods, and our communities. We will hear the first-hand tales of bravery, compassion, and duty within these pages that may inspire the next generation of Latinas in law enforcement.

I am eager to read Michelle's story, and the stories of these heroic Latinas, each told in her own voice.

Sgt. Jo Ann Armenta
Illinois State Police, Retired

INTRODUCTION

As former colleagues and close friends, we—Michelle J. Velasquez and Esmeralda Samaniego—shared a vision that brought this book to life. Our journey into law enforcement has been one of dedication, resilience, service, and purpose. Together, we created this project to highlight the experiences and strength of women in the field. We have joined forces with twelve other incredible Latina women to share our untold stories—fourteen voices from city, state, and federal agencies—united by a shared calling. For each of us, law enforcement is more than just a career, it is a purpose-driven mission.

As Latinas in law enforcement, we have faced obstacles, shattered barriers, and proven time and again that we belong in this field. Through our collective experiences, we hope to inspire, empower, and remind others—especially the next generation—that they, too, can rise to the challenge.

Each chapter in this book tells a different story, yet a common thread ties us all together—perseverance. We come from diverse backgrounds, different cities, and unique life experiences, but we share the same drive, the same struggles, and the same unwavering commitment to serve. Some of us knew from a young age that we wanted to wear the badge, while others found our way here through unexpected turns in life. Regardless of how we arrived, we stand united in our purpose.

Latinas play an essential role in law enforcement. We bring cultural awareness, bilingual skills, and a deep connection to the communities we serve. Our presence fosters trust, improves communication, and ensures fair, respectful interactions, especially in diverse populations. With strong values of hard work, integrity, and resilience, we offer a unique perspective that enhances teamwork, problem-solving, and policy implementation. Most importantly, our representation inspires the next generation, proving that law enforcement is a career where Latinas can lead, protect, and make a lasting impact.

However, this path has not been easy. Being Latinas in law enforcement comes with its own set of challenges. Many of us have had to prove ourselves in ways that others have not. We have faced doubt, stereotypes, and moments of questioning whether we truly belonged. Yet, with every challenge, we have risen stronger, proving that we are not just capable, we are exceptional.

Beyond the uniform, badge and gun, we are wives, daughters, sisters, mothers, friends and most importantly members of the community we serve. We have learned to balance the demands of the job with the responsibilities of our families and personal lives. We have celebrated victories, mourned losses, and leaned on one another in times of need. Through sharing our stories, we hope to provide a glimpse into the realities of our profession—the triumphs, the struggles, and the deep sense of duty that keeps us moving forward.

This book is not just about our individual journeys; it is a testament to the collective strength of Latinas in law enforcement. It is for those who came before us, paving the way and breaking down barriers, so that we could step into these roles with pride. It is for those who stand beside us today, continuing to lead with courage and integrity. And it is for the young women who will follow in our footsteps—the ones who dream of making a difference but may not yet see themselves in this profession.

Some co-authors of this book have chosen not to disclose their department for safety and privacy reasons. We prioritize the safety of all our fellow officers and agents. However, each of these women has proudly served or is currently serving as a sworn officer.

Through these pages, we hope to inspire the next generation, showing them that they are capable, that they are strong, and that they, too, have a place in law enforcement. Our stories are proof that no matter where you come from, with determination and heart, you can achieve greatness.

As you read, we invite you to step into our world, to see law enforcement through our eyes, and to understand the challenges and victories that come with wearing the badge. These are our journeys—stories of courage, sacrifice, and the unbreakable spirit of Latinas in law enforcement.

Welcome to Latinas in Law Enforcement: Stories of Leading with Courage and Breaking Boundaries Beyond the Badge.

From Protecting the Nation to Protecting My Children

MICHELLE J. VELASQUEZ

"Every woman faces a defining moment where she must make a decision that could change her life forever."

My father often spoke of his unfulfilled dream of attending law school, and my mother of her lifelong desire to become a nurse. Their sacrifices and unrealized aspirations instilled in me a deep respect for education and a powerful drive to achieve what they could not. Inspired by their dreams, I pursued a degree in criminal justice at Loyola University Chicago with the intention of going to law school. But by my junior year, I came to a pivotal realization—that dream belonged to my father, not me. It was then that I shifted my focus and set my sights on a career in federal law enforcement, a path that felt truly my own.

As an undergrad, I interned with a federal agency, where a successful assignment on the currency team sparked a passion for protecting the homeland. This led me to pursue a master's degree in criminal administration. In 2007, I applied for and was hired as a federal officer, pausing my studies to attend training at the Federal Law Enforcement Training Center (FLETC).

My time at FLETC was both challenging and rewarding. I was voted class president. As a woman in a predominantly male class, it added a significant amount of pressure, especially as a Latina. I knew I had to prove myself. A defining moment came when a male classmate refused to partner with me because of my gender—yet I succeeded in the training scenario while he failed— powerfully affirming my strength and capability as a Latina in law enforcement. A few months later, I graduated from the academy—one of the happiest moments of my life—as my father proudly pinned my badge, surrounded by my family's unforgettable joy and pride.

After a few months of working at the airport, I came upon a temporary Internal Affairs (IA) detail. Though I was a low-ranking officer, I took a chance. When I asked if I could apply, my chief simply replied, "I don't see why not," giving me the quiet encouragement I needed to move forward with confidence. Working downtown allowed me to ride the train and attend night classes to finish my master's. My three-month

IA assignment stretched longer when another team at the field office needed help, giving me access to leadership and new opportunities. A highlight while working at the field office was escorting Commissioner W. Ralph Basham during his Chicago visit. I shared my ideas—he appreciated my honesty—and later launched a virtual course based on them. It showed me the power of speaking up.

In 2008, I became head advisor for the Explorer Program, mentoring youth interested in law enforcement. I prioritized recruiting inner-city kids and was honored with the Advisor of the Year award, nominated by my students. Many later became officers, giving me valuable connections across departments—a simple call to a former explorer often made all the difference.

As a Latina, I was raised to believe that hard work always pays off. But I also learned that this is not always true. While at the field office, I encountered a moment where my hard work held me back. There was a perfect opportunity for a temporary assignment. I eagerly applied for the position, but when I didn't hear back, I asked an upper manager about it. Her response stunned me: "I didn't submit your name." When I asked why, she said, "Who would run the Explorers if you left?"

That moment was a revelation, and it changed my perspective and attitude forever. My success in volunteering and excelling had unintentionally become a barrier to growing professionally. People wanted to pigeonhole me because it benefited them, even though it was holding me back from growth. When I realized this, I made the tough decision to step away from running the

Explorers Program. It was a painful decision after all the effort I had given; however, I was not going to be hindered from moving forward.

In my final year of grad school, I interned with High Intensity Drug Trafficking Area (HIDTA) while working full time and attending night classes. It pushed me to the limit, but I never quit. I graduated in 2009 and joined a team handling cases with legal permanent residents. Being a Latina was critical—many cases required Spanish, and I saw firsthand how attorneys exploited people's language barriers and lack of knowledge. It infuriated me and deepened my commitment to justice.

I made it my mission to ensure that these individuals understood their cases fully and weren't left in the dark. I took pride in ensuring that they were informed, treated with respect, and understood the difference between criminal and immigration proceedings. The attorneys hated dealing with me because they knew I didn't tolerate nonsense.

As a Latina in law enforcement, I often heard people, "How could a Latina work for the feds?" They didn't realize how crucial it is to have Latinas in the federal government—people who truly care. When families need help with documentation, when language barriers arise, or when policies need explaining, we are there. Our presence isn't just about translation—it's about cultural awareness, strong values, and a deep commitment to serving our communities. Latinas are indispensable in law enforcement, both for the agency and the people we protect.

In October 2010, my father passed away. His loss hit me

hard, and I struggled to cope. The only way I knew to escape my reality was to throw myself into something new. Around that time, our agency was recruiting instructors to teach at FLETC. Since I loved teaching, it felt like the perfect opportunity, so I packed my bags and moved to Saint Simons Island, Georgia.

In 2011, God changed my life when I met my husband, Martin. Shortly after we started dating, I had to leave for FLETC. I told him it was only a six-month detail, and he flew monthly to visit. When my assignment ended, I was offered a six-month extension and a chance for permanency. I broke the news to Martin, and he wasn't thrilled. He gave me an ultimatum. He told me, "You have to decide whether you're going to gain more or lose more by staying another six months. You decide what you want."

I believe every woman faces a defining moment where she must make a decision that could change her life forever—this was mine. There was something special about Martin. I loved that he's a God-fearing, family-oriented, highly educated Latino—and a bit of a nerd. But building a life together mattered most; so I packed my bags and he drove us home.

Shortly after returning to Chicago, we got pregnant. In law enforcement, pregnancy meant light duty—which I thought I'd hate, but I thrived. I applied to the Border Security Team covering the Midwest, my dream job. For the first time, I had a Monday-Friday schedule downtown.

I had amazing leadership and a team I hoped to retire with. It was the only unit based on skill, not seniority, and it opened my eyes to our agency's potential. We worked closely with outside agencies, and I was one of only two women—and the only Latina. Our managers trusted us to lead, and for the first time, I could fully use my gifts.

In 2012, I received a surprise call from Secretary Janet Napolitano after submitting cost-saving ideas for the Think Efficiency Campaign. While others ignored it, I took it seriously, and she personally reached out to discuss my suggestions. That experience showed me the power of speaking up.

While on the Dream Team, I became a mom. When Marty, my oldest, started at a dual-language school, my rigid work hours made it hard to support him. My request for flexibility was denied, so I pulled him out, not wanting to seem "difficult" or "special" because I was a mom. I regret not fighting harder for his Spanish—it's key to our roots.

Then came Izan and Joe, and life got busier. I started driving instead of taking the train for more flexibility with daycare, school, and errands. Sports soon packed our schedule. Juggling it all was tough, but I kept adapting. As a Latina mom, kids come first—so my career took a backseat, and I didn't apply for any details or promotions.

In 2018, I had one of the most unforgettable moments of my career. One of the supervisors I was helping on a case submitted an award and my team and I were invited to the White House to receive the US Interdiction Coordinator (USIC) Award. That recognition symbolized the power of teamwork and the impact of multi-agency collaboration.

In 2020, when COVID-19 hit the world, I was pregnant with my fourth child. It was a time of fear and uncertainty; but in May 2020, Adaleah was born, and she changed everything. Suddenly, I wasn't just a mom of boys—I had a daughter. For some reason, having a girl felt different. I felt the need to protect her. I felt this huge responsibility to do better, knowing I was going to have a little shadow watching my every move. Adaleah was a gift from God and exactly what our family needed.

During my maternity leave, COVID-19 was at its peak, and with an autoimmune disease, the uncertainty was terrifying. As a mom of four, the pandemic pushed my exhaustion to new limits. Virtual school lasted just an hour, leaving me to homeschool Marty (seven), teach Izan (four), chase Joe (two), and nurse a newborn—while also trying to "save the country." This experience gave me a new perspective on motherhood and appreciation for my husband who was previously carrying the load.

On Marty's first day back to school after the pandemic, I stood at the front door as he got on the bus. He turned around, waved, and said, "Bye, Mommy." At that moment, it hit me— where had time gone? My baby wasn't a baby anymore; he was seven years old. As I closed the door, I broke down in tears. That moment forever changed my life. It made me redefine what I truly valued, my family. I felt like so many years had been stolen. I had been so focused on saving the country that I was losing sight of my own children. That realization shook me to my core. I knew that others could help save the country, but only I could save my kids.

This was the beginning of my mental struggle. I knew deep down that God wanted me to stay home with my kids. For a while, I tried to convince myself otherwise, pretending I wasn't completely sure of His plan. In the midst of this internal battle, I experienced the heartbreaking loss of my stillborn niece, Celeste. Her loss taught me a valuable lesson: cherish the present moments. I've always struggled with being fully present as a mother, but Celeste's memory is a daily reminder to prioritize my family.

Ironically, during this time, I received an opportunity for a collateral assignment to help the Workforce Team—a group focused on supporting our employees. Yet I was feeling completely incapable of helping myself. "Mom guilt" was consuming me. Though I'd always given 150 percent, this season left me drained, overwhelmed with guilt and tears at my desk, until a light switched on—I couldn't ignore it. So, I turned to God, praying for clarity and direction.

One sleepless night, I felt God speaking to me, telling me it was time to take the leap. He made it clear: if I didn't obey, I would be pushed out. It was time to leave the job I had loved for so many years. Being an officer had become my identity. I felt God was asking me to sacrifice what I loved most, my career.

I remember heading to the shooting range with my colleague, Frank. When the targets turned, I missed several shots. After sixteen years, I failed for the first time. At that moment, all I heard was God saying, *You don't belong here anymore. I've called you to leave.* When asked if I wanted to try again, I said "No." I knew it wasn't my aim, it was my struggle with obedience. That day was the final sign. After talking with my husband and pastor, it was clear; if God was calling me out, I had to follow.

Before resigning, I delayed training ten officers in the financial wellness program I had long advocated for. After fulfilling that promise, I submitted my resignation to focus on my children and the mother I aspired to be. At the same time, I felt God calling me to grow Virtuous Wealth Building, my financial coaching business, helping overwhelmed moms gain confidence and control over their finances after seeing the struggles brought on by COVID-19.

It dawned on me that this was how I could continue to give back, how I could fulfill my purpose while being present for my kids. It hasn't been easy. I'll never feel like a "normal civilian." Every time an incident makes the news; I can't help but wonder if I could have made a difference had I stayed. But I know I'm where I'm supposed to be. I am walking in my purpose. God's calling was clear, and I'm walking in obedience—trusting Him to guide my path.

Being a federal law enforcement officer was an extraordinary honor. If I could choose again, I would proudly serve. Every time I put on the uniform, I gave it my best and wore it with pride. I was privileged to work alongside exceptional people. Leaving that career was one of the hardest decisions I've made, but my gratitude remains for those who selflessly protect and serve.

As a proud Latina, I carry those experiences with me. While many brave souls protect our country, only I can protect my children—and that is my greatest calling.

To the women aspiring to join law enforcement—be proud to be the FIRST, and sometimes the ONLY. Remember, never leave your values and morals at the door. Bring them with you, always.

A MOMENT OF IMPACT IN LAW ENFORCEMENT

My moment of impact came when I helped a local agency solve a decades-old case, leading to the arrest of a suspect who had evaded justice for nearly twenty years. As a mother of four, the case felt deeply personal. I was grateful to help bring peace and closure to that family—a powerful reminder of why I chose this path: to protect, to serve, and to make a lasting difference.

A Childhood Dream: My Journey into Law Enforcement

ESMERALDA SAMANIEGO

———

"I didn't want to be on the sidelines anymore—I wanted to be part of the solution, part of something bigger than myself."

From a young age, I dreamt of serving in law enforcement. Playing cops and robbers with my siblings sparked a passion that never faded. To be honest, the dream wasn't initially mine—it was my brother and sisters' dream—but they planted the seed, and I ran with it.

I was born and raised in Chicago to Mexican parents, Maria de Jesus and Jose Armando Samaniego. I came from a large family with eleven siblings. My mother and father had four children together, and I am the second oldest. We were the first generation born in the United States, and I didn't learn English until I was seven years old. Though we had a middle-class upbringing, my father worked tirelessly to put us in Catholic school—his way of keeping us from becoming "gangbangers." He was strict, traditional, and firm in his beliefs. We rarely questioned him, mostly out of fear. My mother was a stay-at-home mom but just as hard-working. She cooked three meals a day, did all the laundry, and kept the house spotless. To me, she was an angel on earth. People believed she had the gift of healing, and I witnessed it firsthand.

My siblings are my life. My older sister, Yesenia, was my first best friend, my mentor. I idolized her so much I dressed like her for years. My brother, Jorge Armando, grew up surrounded by three sisters and went along with everything we did, developing a great sense of humor and a huge heart. We aren't twins, but we look so much alike that we started calling each other "twins." Then there's Cindy, the glue that holds us together. She talks to all of us daily and keeps us connected—we call her "the bridge." At fifteen, I gained another brother, Jose Antonio, when my father invited him to be a *chambelán* for my *Quinceañera* introducing him to us for the first time. He fit in seamlessly. It was like gaining a new best friend, but even better, because he was our brother. My older siblings from my father's side lived in other states, so I didn't grow up much with them, but I love them just the same. Thanks to social media, we now stay in touch.

Our lives changed when my father had a stroke at fifty-seven, and my mother became his full-time caregiver for twenty-three years. In 2020, she was diagnosed with Alzheimer's. Within a year, she went from forgetting simple tasks to forgetting our names. Watching her decline has been one of the hardest things we've faced. This is why I decided to write this, because I owe it to them—to their struggles, sacrifices, and unfulfilled dreams.

Growing up in Chicago in the 1980s, I had little guidance. My neighborhood was rough, and many kids struggled to stay on the right path. Police sirens were heard every day and night, they often woke us up from deep sleep. Gang violence and crime were common, but our backyard became a safe haven. My father built a fence topped with barbed wire to keep others from jumping in and out. We formed close bonds with our neighbors, friendships that have lasted a lifetime. Much of our childhood was spent playing basketball, riding bikes, and kicking a soccer ball in the alley. But no one talked about education or careers.

Being first-generation in the United States, I often felt lost about my future. I surrounded myself with career-driven friends, following their lead—attending the same high school and applying to the same universities. My mother was always supportive, wanting the best for my future. My father, on the other hand, didn't see the need for me to pursue higher education. Our family owned two small businesses, and he expected us to dedicate ourselves to them. In his eyes, women weren't meant to be taken seriously in the workforce, we belonged at home or working in his business.

My siblings made a tremendous sacrifice. When my father became disabled, they took over the family business so I could focus on my education. Over time, his mindset changed. As he watched me reach goal after goal, his criticism faded. The man who once told me I'd "shoot myself in the foot" because I was a woman in law enforcement became one of my biggest supporters.

Pursuing this career wasn't easy. My choices profoundly affected my family. We were all so young; my oldest sister was just twenty-one, and I was only eighteen when my father's health declined. The family business became our lifeline, and my siblings carried that weight so I could chase my dream. Their belief in me motivated me to persevere. Their sacrifice is something I will always carry in my heart.

In 1998, while juggling school and family responsibilities, I managed to graduate from high school. That same summer I joined the American Airlines Academy, leading to a job at O'Hare International Airport as a customer service representative for *Mexicana de Aviación*. For five years, my job wasn't just about issuing tickets, boarding passengers at the gate, and dealing with oversold flights, I often found myself serving as a translator for federal law enforcement agencies. Every time I assisted a federal officer, I felt a pull towards something greater, something more meaningful. I knew that I could be of great assistance in the community and build a bridge between law enforcement and the people, my people, the Latinos.

Then, September 11, 2001, happened. I still remember exactly where I was that morning. Sitting in my room, finishing a homework assignment, when the breaking news flashed across my TV screen. At first, it didn't seem real. The images of the Twin Towers collapsing, the panic, the sheer devastation—it was unlike anything I had ever witnessed. And just like that, the world stood still. Flights were grounded, security tightened, and the entire country entered a state of mourning and fear. That day when I arrived for work at O'Hare everything was still. The sense of helplessness changed everything for me. Watching the tragedy unfold fueled a determination in me to serve. I didn't want to be on the sidelines anymore—I wanted to be part of the solution, part of something bigger than myself.

Not long after, many federal law enforcement agencies began to hire. It felt like a sign. I had been assisting officers at O'Hare for years, but this was my opportunity to take the next step. Without hesitation, I attended an open house and applied. I was only twenty-one years old, full of ambition and nerves, but deep down I knew this was the path I was meant to take.

The hiring process was rigorous and took nearly two years. Background checks, interviews, physical tests—it was a long and uncertain road. But in 2003, the call finally came. I had been selected.

The timing couldn't have been more perfect. That same summer, I graduated from the University of Illinois Chicago with my bachelor's degree in accounting. Just weeks after walking across the stage to receive my diploma, I packed my bags and left for the Federal Law Enforcement Training Center (FLETC), where I would spend the next four months in intensive training.

This was the first time that I ever spent away from my family. I had no prior law enforcement experience, no real idea of what awaited me at the academy. Everything I knew, I would learn there—how to handle a firearm, how to conduct arrests, how to protect and serve.

I had dreamed of this moment since I was a little girl, playing with my brother and sisters, cops and robbers. And now, standing on the threshold of my career, I was finally stepping into the future I had always imagined.

Upon returning from the academy, I'm not going to lie, there was fear of failure; I was scared of the unknown. The first few months felt long and tiresome, working long shifts and learning the job. It was almost depressing reporting to work. But I learned quickly that being a Latina, Spanish speaker, and female gave me an advantage. There was a high demand for my skillset, and I quickly joined enforcement teams. Just a year in, I found myself on specialized tactical units—dream assignments for many officers.

For nearly twenty years, I worked on cases involving terrorism, child exploitation, money laundering, narcotics, human trafficking, and smuggling. The work was intense, exposing me to the darkest parts of society. Over time, I saw firsthand the toll these investigations took on officers—the trauma, stress, and silent battles they faced.

After two decades in enforcement, I made one of the biggest decisions of my career—stepping back from frontline operations to focus on those who serve. Transitioning from high-intensity enforcement teams to my current role as a program manager wasn't easy, but I now dedicate myself to officers' wellness and mental health, leading initiatives that ensure those who protect others are also protected. I am now the program manager over many units, like recruitment, honor guard, explorers, peer support, and chaplains, to name a few. I also oversee community outreach efforts. Something that I felt was so important. "Why?" you may ask. Well, representation matters.

In many Latino cultures, there is a deep-rooted fear of the police. I grew up hearing, "Behave, or the police will come get you," which planted seeds of fear. Even as an officer, I sometimes feel that same nervousness when I see a patrol car behind me. My family and friends still yell, "¡La policia!" out of habit. It's a mindset ingrained in our community, and I wanted it to change.

Having Latinas in law enforcement is crucial because we can help bridge that gap, showing our communities that officers serve to protect, not instill fear. Representation matters, especially for children who grow up with misconceptions. I often talk to my nieces and nephews and let them see me in uniform, so they associate law enforcement with trust, not fear. One of my proudest moments is when they ask, "Tía, are you the police?" I love knowing that they look up to me.

Having mentors in law enforcement is crucial. I have been blessed with mentors along the way, individuals who saw something in me before I saw it in myself. My mentors have pushed me beyond my comfort zone. Sometimes they threw me into the fire, challenging me in ways I didn't understand at the time. But every challenge, every test, prepared me for the leader I have become today. To them, I say: Thank you. Thanks to them, I also became a mentor.

For nearly twenty years, I've mentored countless young boys and girls through the Explorer Program, introducing them to law enforcement careers. I dedicated every Thursday evening to the program, often sacrificing vacations and personal time. Seeing young people look up to me and pursue their dreams has made every effort worthwhile. I've had the honor of pinning badges and attending graduations for former Explorers, who are now officers. Officers who have now become friends.

Many of the friendships from work became family. Many have guided me, becoming my role models and lifelong friends. Their resilience inspires me daily. We share struggles we often don't talk about enough, such as the toll this career takes on our bodies. The weight of 20-pound belts, 10-pound vests, and heavy gear adds up over time, leading to back pain, aching feet, and long-term injuries. Younger me would be proud that I've learned to speak openly about these challenges. I've been called Wonder Woman throughout my career, but even Wonder Woman has her battles.

Every struggle, every sacrifice, every victory, and every friendship has shaped me into who I am today. My journey hasn't been easy, but it has been worth every step. Being a Latina in law enforcement isn't just a career, it's a calling. And I am proud to answer that call every single day. Because if I—a Latina girl from Chicago, raised in a strict household, with no guidance or mentorship—can do it, so can you.

A MOMENT OF IMPACT IN LAW ENFORCEMENT

In every law enforcement career, there are defining moments that shape us. For me, that moment came when I decided to join the Explorer Program at twenty-four. Fresh-faced and uncertain about my path, I had no idea this decision would lay the foundation for my career.

Mentoring young Explorers became my "why." I saw myself in them—lost and seeking direction. As I grew alongside them, I found fulfillment in watching their success and realized that this program was more than just a way to give back; it was my purpose. Every leadership drill, every challenge, made me a better officer and leader.

Through the Explorer Program, I discovered a passion for mentorship that led me to join the Honor Guard, where I climbed the ranks from being yelled "Samaniego" repeatedly in the Honor Guard Academy, to becoming the Chicago Field Office Honor Guard commander.

Though I'm still in my career, I worry about who will carry these programs with so much love and dedication forward. My greatest hope is that another young officer will step into my role, embrace the opportunities, and find their own moment of impact. In the end, the true measure of our careers is not just in our achievements, but in the lives we touch and the legacy we leave behind.

A Direction in Life: Determination

MY CHAVEZ

"I don't care to be a 'hero,' I just want to do good in this life. If I can help, then I will."

If you were to ask someone that works in law enforcement, why they wanted to become a police officer, many might say it was a dream of theirs since they were young. Others might say it is because they have always wanted to be in a position to help others, saving lives during the most dangerous moments and worst situations. If I am being brutally honest, I cannot give you an answer. I have pondered on this question for many years and have yet to come up with a solid response. It might be that I drew inspiration from someone close to me, my better half.

I do believe that a big part of why I became a police officer is because of the passion I saw within him. His dream, for the longest time, had been to become a police officer. He worked extremely hard and sacrificed so much to achieve that goal. Throughout the years of knowing him, I have seen the selfless acts he has done for his family, friends, and even myself. He is the type of person that will give you his last dollar, the shoes on his feet, without question. A person like that is extremely rare in today's world. He is the true definition of what someone born to become a police officer is. I am extremely lucky and grateful to be a part of that and we both get to grow together. Every day we strive to do the best that we can with what life has given us, never taking things for granted. For me, becoming a police officer just felt right. That is the only way I can explain it. I really do not see myself doing anything else. Even on the hardest of days, the longest of nights, it just feels like this is something I should be doing.

I grew up in a large family—nine bodies in one household. My parents had their hands full making sure we had a roof over our head and food on the table. My parents migrated to the United States with nothing, yet they worked extremely hard to make sure we had a place to lay our heads down at night. We did not grow up with much. All we knew at the time was work. My parents lived to work. From the moment they opened their eyes to the moment they laid in bed it was work 24/7, for years and years. They were trying their best to survive and provide for us. Unfortunately, because of that mindset they sometimes forgot to enjoy life. The years just passed them by as they unselfishly worked tirelessly every day. I knew that I didn't want to live this way. I wanted more from life. The question was, what and how do I get to where I want to be in order to have a well-balanced life.

After leaving home, I had many moments of uncertainty on whether I could make it or not. I found myself without an official home at times, asking friends to sleep on the floor for a few days until I could get back on my feet and a place of my own. I would ride the trains for hours because I had nowhere else to go. I did not want to be a burden to anyone or ask for any more help than I had already asked from people. I would stay at school for as long as I could, showering at the gym, and hardly eating because I barely had enough money to get by. I tried my best to keep up with my academics, attending class, and maintaining two to three jobs at a time to afford the bare minimum. Ultimately, I had to drop out of college to work and to provide for myself.

Throughout all the years I kept taking classes on and off. I taught myself how to bake cakes and cupcakes. With the help of my amazing family and friends I would set up a little table in a busy intersection to sell my cupcakes with a sign that would say, "Cupcakes for College," to pay for college classes and schoolbooks. After so many years of going to school on and off, I was finally able to obtain a bachelor's degree in 2023. A small feat for some, but for me, I could not be prouder having my mother, boyfriend, and best friends watch me cross that stage. I stood tall and proud with tears in my eyes because everyone there was a testament to how hard I had worked and struggled to get to that point. I had finally achieved that special moment and attained that educational goal.

I think the struggles that I have witnessed and endured in life have been my most valuable asset on this job. It has given me an understanding and an empathetic point of view for my fellow man in need of help. I would say I have a peaceful home, an amazing partner, two amazing step-children, and two loving dogs that have helped me de-stress. My home is my sanctuary, my safe space, and I firmly believe that I can be a safe space for someone that is in need. Everyone deserves peace. I want to provide safety and peace for those that call the police for help in their moment of need.

Many of us grow up seeing and living through things that no human being should. We cannot control what happens to us, but it is our own responsibility to learn and heal from it. Moments like these have a huge impact on how you perceive life and how you choose to live it. It can either break you or motivate you enough to push through it. In saying that, certain things do matter when a person is dealing with some of the worst moments of their life. I realized that sometimes just your presence, as a law enforcement officer, can have such a positive impact on someone. Maybe you stopped them from ending their own lives. You talked to them and made them feel heard, having them realize that they are not alone. You can show them that there is another way out of any situation. I hope that I have been that helping hand to others.

Law enforcement today is one of the most challenging jobs to be in. Just by wearing the uniform alone you will be treated like you are the worst person in the world and be called the vilest names you've ever heard. People can forget that you are human, too. Many will dislike you for it, but will never understand it unless they have experienced and seen what police officers have to witness every day. A mistake can cost you your life or your freedom.

Getting into law enforcement was not an easy task. In such a male-dominated profession, it can be quite challenging for females to get in and want to stay in. I don't care much to compare sexes or races because, at the end of the day, we all need each other. In the end, no matter who you are or where you come from, you are part of this family and we will always have your back when you need help.

As a female on the job, I have been able to contribute a different perspective to my peers. Many tend to feel more comfortable speaking to female officers, rather than male officers. I have been able to de-escalate situations that could have gotten bad or violent. Some of the challenges as a female police officer is that you can be perceived as physically weaker than your male peers. You become an easier target if someone wants to do harm. It is extremely important on this job to stay fit, stand your ground, and hold your own. Unfortunately, it feels like you have to work twice as hard to prove that you can do the job as well as anyone else.

Knowing two languages has helped me immensely on this job. It's a great tool for finding common ground in a community with a language barrier. The community feels heard and represented and cuts the stigma of "us" versus "them." We create a stronger connection to your community and are willing to open up more and talk.

I have had the honor of working with some of the most amazing, baddest, and bravest women I have ever met in my life. Women I strive to be when I grow up. These women are the greatest example of a role model on the job, a true friend, and what a support system should be. I look at my friends and admire each and every one of them because they each bring something different to the table. Each and every one of them make amazing police officers and deserve the very best. We have fought side by side without giving it a second thought. The friendships I have made are worth more than gold.

As dangerous as it is, why do I continue loving and doing the job that I do? Never in my life have I ever met so many people of different backgrounds, races, and life experiences. People of different age groups and different points of view in life working together. We can dislike each other, disagree or argue, but at the end of the day, if you need help, we are there by your side without question. Once that uniform is on and that oath to protect and to serve has been made, we have each other's back no matter what.

Never in my life have I experienced anyone willing to take a bullet for one another like I have here. I have found another family here. We are all human and want to go home safe to our families. This career has exposed me to some of the worst moments and some of the best experiences I have ever had. I wouldn't change it for the world. I don't care to be a "hero," I just want to do good in this life. If I can help, then I will. It doesn't hurt to be kind. We, as human beings, need to do better in this world.

A MOMENT OF IMPACT IN LAW ENFORCEMENT

One of the most impactful moments in my law enforcement career was during the end of a service call. A man that I had translated for, approached me speaking in Spanish, and said how he was so happy to see me again. He shook my hand with tears in his eyes and stated that he hoped that he would run into me one day. He said, "Thanks to you, because of your advice, my daughter is getting help and doing better."

It was then that I realized how important it is to be in the position that I am in. It is so important to treat everyone fairly and with kindness, even when it isn't reciprocated. Sometimes it's little moments like these that can have the most impact and confirm to you that you are doing something good.

BIOGRAPHY

My Chavez was born and raised in the beautiful city of Chicago. She is the middle child out of seven. Although she initially went to college in the art field, My graduated from Calumet College of St. Joseph with a bachelor's degree for public safety management. My was thirty years old when she finally got the opportunity to start her law enforcement career. She has been working in law enforcement since June 2016. She has worked as a patrol officer for most of her career.

My Chavez has encountered many moments of uncertainty and danger within her field but has also witnessed some of the most amazing, resilient people because of her job. This career in law enforcement has been a blessing and she only hopes that she can further expand her knowledge and experiences to make it further into her career.

My has a love for photography and animals, which is a great way to escape and mentally recharge from the stresses of the job. Only time will tell where her career choice will lead, but she hopes that she can still help people and make a bit of a difference—be the light in someone's darkest moment.

My Chavez
Mygraphix12@yahoo.com

Resilient Superwoman in Blue

AMANDA B. CRUZ

"That realization fueled my desire to make a difference not just as an officer but as someone who could inspire young Latinas to pursue their dreams, no matter how difficult they might seem."

Never in a million years did I think I would be sitting here, writing and sharing my story as a Latina in law enforcement. I was approached by my good friend, Michelle Velasquez, who is the author of this book. She had the brilliant idea of starting an anthology featuring the voices of Latinas in law enforcement. As she described the project, my eyes lit up like a Christmas tree, and my heart began to race as I drifted into a daydream, where I was sitting at a table, signing autographs with paparazzi surrounding me. Michelle went on to explain the logistics, and I was completely sold. With bubbling enthusiasm, I told her to sign me up right away!

I was born and raised in Chicago. Growing up, I lived in a middle-class household with my hardworking parents and my younger siblings. As the eldest child, I had responsibilities early on; but it wasn't until later in life that I realized how much my parents' resilience had shaped me. My father worked three jobs at one point, and my mother balanced a full-time job while raising us and managing our home. Watching them work tirelessly to provide for our family instilled in me the values of dedication and perseverance.

In high school, I was a solid B student—not at the top, not at the bottom, just comfortable in the middle. I enjoyed sports, had a strong group of friends, and, like many teenagers, was still finding my way. However, it wasn't until I went to college that I began to find a deeper sense of purpose. I started my college journey at Northern Illinois University, where I joined Sigma Lambda Gamma National Sorority, Inc. That decision shaped my college experience and, in many ways, the woman I've become. Through Sigma Lambda Gamma, I found a sisterhood that empowered me to be strong, independent, and a leader. Our motto was one of strength, unity, and perseverance—qualities that have helped me navigate the many challenges in my life.

It was during my time at Northern that my life took a turn in more ways than one. I found myself in a difficult situation; I was a victim of domestic violence. The relationship was emotionally draining and physically threatening to the point where I almost died. But I survived it. That experience left a lasting impact on me. It broke me down in ways I had never imagined, but it also built me up in ways I didn't expect. Surviving that relationship helped shape and mold me into the strong, determined woman I am today.

I often reflect on how that chapter in my life brought me closer to my purpose. It taught me resilience, how to stand my ground, and how to reclaim my power when it feels like everything is slipping away. Being involved in a domestic violence situation wasn't something I ever saw for myself, but as painful as it was, it made me more compassionate and aware of the struggles others face behind closed doors.

Around the same time, I also had a beautiful baby girl, Marie. Becoming a mother was one of the most transformative experiences of my life. Everything shifted, and suddenly, my priorities were laser-focused on my daughter. As any parent knows, raising a child while trying to pursue higher education is no easy feat, but I was determined to build a future for us. This dual experience surviving an abusive relationship and stepping into motherhood gave me a new perspective on life. It solidified my understanding of what true strength looks like. It's not about how much you can endure but how you rebuild yourself after being torn apart. These experiences made me who I am today, fueling my drive to make a difference, not just for myself but for my daughter and for others who might be going through similar hardships.

After giving birth to Marie, I made the decision to transfer to DePaul University to complete my degree. DePaul offered a different environment and opportunities that aligned more with my evolving goals. It was there that I earned my undergraduate degree, a milestone that not only signified my academic achievements but also my resilience as a mother, student, and Latina.

I didn't always plan to become a police officer. In fact, if you had asked me in my early twenties, I wouldn't have had a clear answer for what I wanted to do. All I wanted was to graduate with my business degree and own some kind of business. But my family, particularly my mother, planted the seeds. My mom was the first person to send me links and reminders whenever law enforcement applications opened. She thought this career would be stable for me. After all, I was raising a beautiful baby girl on my own. I also was working in sales, which were commission-only jobs. In 2012, when I first applied, the city wasn't hiring often, and the process seemed frozen for years. I wasn't even that interested at the time I applied. Mostly, I wanted to make my mother happy.

I took the written exam and passed it. But then came the physical test and I failed. Not just once or twice, but three times. Each failure discouraged me more, and after the third time, I decided I was done. I wasn't going to apply again. I had other plans, other dreams, and frankly, I didn't see myself fitting into that world.

In 2017, something shifted. The opportunity to apply came up again, and I found myself questioning whether it was too late. I was thirty-one years old. Would I even pass the fitness test? But I had been working out more consistently and eating healthier, so I decided to give it one more shot. To my surprise, I passed not only the written exam but the fitness test as well. By 2018, I found myself in the police academy, stepping into a whole new world, one I never thought I would be a part of.

The decision to pursue law enforcement was not just a personal one. It impacted my entire family, especially Marie. Finding babysitters and adjusting to the unpredictable schedule was one of the hardest parts of the transition. My parents, siblings, and extended family all rallied around me, helping where they could. I had to quickly adapt to a lifestyle where I was balancing police training, studying, and being a mom. There were days when I wasn't sure I could handle the weight of it all, but with the support of my family and the encouragement of my sorority sisters, I kept pushing forward.

Being a Latina in law enforcement has opened my eyes in many ways. Growing up in Chicago, I was always surrounded by diversity, but when I entered the police force, I was struck by how underrepresented Latinas were in this field. That realization fueled my desire to make a difference not just as an officer but as someone who could inspire young Latinas to pursue their dreams, no matter how difficult they might seem.

Alongside my law enforcement career, I also embarked on a new venture and started my real estate business, determined to build something of my own and provide for my family in multiple ways. Balancing these two careers has been challenging, but it also has been incredibly fulfilling. I've found that both professions allow me to help people, whether it's through protecting and serving my community or helping families find their dream homes.

As a Latina, I bring more to the table than just my ability to speak Spanish. I bring cultural awareness and an understanding of the communities I serve. My background allows me to connect with people on a deeper level, to understand their struggles and needs, and to build trust. The bond I've created with the communities I serve is something I hold dear, and it's a big part of why I continue to do this work, even on the hardest days.

Mentorship is a crucial part of my life journey, and I believe it's incredibly important for Latinas in law enforcement to have mentors they can relate to. Though I didn't have many Latina mentors in the academy, I was fortunate to find mentorship within the districts. Experienced officers—some Latina, some not—helped guide me through the challenges of the job. These mentors offered crucial advice, helping me understand the intricacies of law enforcement and the unwritten rules that come with the job. They shared their wisdom, passed down from years of experience, and helped me develop the confidence to handle tough situations. It was through these district mentors that I began to find my footing, and I'm incredibly grateful for their support.

Having a Latina mentor, in particular, someone who looked

like me, who understood both the cultural pressures and the professional expectations, could have helped me navigate the often-intimidating environment. It's hard enough breaking into a male-dominated field, but being a Latina adds another layer of complexity. If I had had a Latina mentor during that time, it would have been a game-changer. She would have been someone to relate to on a cultural level, offering advice—not only on how to handle the job but also on how to maintain balance between family expectations and career ambitions.

Latina mentors offer a special kind of support, not only because of their shared experiences but because they serve as living proof that we can thrive in this field. They help bridge the gap for young officers, making the transition into law enforcement smoother and more supportive. My mentors showed me how to approach the job with both professionalism and heart, and they also taught me the importance of giving back by mentoring others. I believe that having strong Latina mentors creates a ripple effect of empowerment throughout the department. When you see someone who looks like you succeeding, it gives you the confidence to push through barriers and achieve your own goals. That's why I'm so committed to mentoring younger officers today, so they can feel supported, encouraged, and confident in their abilities to succeed.

Law enforcement also has gifted me with some of the most important friendships of my life. The bonds you form with your colleagues in this line of work are unlike anything else. When you spend 12-hour shifts together, work festival details for an entire week, or handle tense situations side by side, you become more than coworkers—you become family. One of my closest friends today, who I now consider a sister, is someone I met during some of the toughest moments of my career. She's helped me grow both personally and professionally, teaching me to think differently, listen more carefully, and approach challenges with a calm and clear mind. And let me tell you, her faith keeps her strong, and that energy is contagious.

Despite the strong bonds and personal growth, being a Latina in law enforcement is not without its challenges. Some of the difficulties are the everyday, practical issues like standing on a street corner in 80-degree heat while wearing 30 pounds of equipment or struggling to find a restroom in establishments that aren't always welcoming to police officers. Then there's the added challenge of being one of the few women on a shift. There were countless times when I'd be called across the city because the dispatcher needed a Spanish-speaking female officer. The workload piles up quickly in those situations, and it can feel overwhelming.

But even with these challenges, I always remind myself why I chose this path. My parents worked so hard to give me and my siblings a better life, and I want to show my daughter that you can achieve anything you set your mind to, no matter your age, your ethnic background, or your circumstances. My family's sacrifices drive me to keep going, and the motto I've held onto from my sorority days continues to push me forward: "What doesn't kill me, only makes me stronger."

In this career, I've learned that law enforcement isn't just about enforcing the law. It's about serving with empathy and understanding. I try to approach every situation with my heart as much as my mind. When I listen to people, I don't just hear their words, I try to understand their feelings, their fears, and their needs. I believe that's what sets me apart, and that's what makes this job more than just a paycheck or a career. It's a calling to serve, to protect, and to make a real impact on the lives of others.

Looking back on my journey, I feel an overwhelming sense of gratitude. Grateful for my family, my mentors, and my sorority sisters, who all encouraged me to keep pushing forward. Grateful for the opportunity to serve my community and to inspire other young Latinas to follow their dreams. Most of all, grateful that I've had the chance to lead with my heart, stay true to my roots, and pave the way for others. *!Sí se puede!*

A MOMENT OF IMPACT IN LAW ENFORCEMENT

In 2020—the year of chaos and uncertainty—it was a trial by fire for law enforcement. One day, in particular, is seared into my memory. My partner and I had just started our shift when urgent calls flooded the radio with multiple "10-1" distress signals—officers needed immediate assistance.

We rerouted to Madison and Kedzie, where unrest had erupted. Even before arriving, we could hear the chaos, screams, shattering glass, and the relentless thud of projectiles. As we stepped out of the squad car, a wave of hostility met us. Bottles and bricks rained down. My hands trembled as I gripped my baton, heart pounding. My partner, always steady, looked just as shaken.

Minutes stretched into eternity. The line between order and anarchy blurred as we fought to hold our ground. A brick barely missed my head. A bottle shattered at my feet. Between clenched teeth, I whispered desperate prayers.

Finally, reinforcements arrived. Slowly, control was restored. When it was over, I collapsed into my seat, drained. That shift changed me. It revealed the raw reality of this job, the fear, the courage, and the resilience it demands. I will carry that moment with me forever.

BIOGRAPHY

Amanda B. Cruz is a proud Latina, dedicated police officer, real estate agent, and travel agent, skillfully balancing multiple roles with grace and determination. Born and raised in Chicago, she is a devoted mother to her beautiful daughter, Marie. Amanda's journey has been one of resilience and perseverance, deeply influenced by her experiences as a domestic violence survivor. This challenging chapter in her life has shaped her into the strong, compassionate woman she is today, fueling her passion for helping others.

As a police officer, Amanda is committed to serving and protecting her community, working tirelessly to foster trust and understanding between law enforcement and the diverse populations she serves. In addition to her work in law enforcement, she is a skilled real estate agent who helps families find their dream homes and a travel agent who curates unforgettable experiences for her clients.

Beyond her professional endeavors, Amanda is a loving daughter and sister, always supporting her family. She actively mentors young Latinas, inspiring them to pursue their dreams and reminding them that they are capable of achieving anything. Amanda's unwavering commitment to her family and community defines her inspiring story and legacy.

Amanda B. Cruz
amandabcruz2022@gmail.com
IG: @amanda_b_cruz

From Piecing It Together to Inner Peace

GUADALUPE JASSO

"You don't have to have it all figured out to take the first step. Sometimes a piece comes one piece at a time."

My journey began with my mother. She worked at a small family-owned factory that appeared to be a modest two-flat apartment building from the outside, on the North Side of Chicago. Inside, it was something unexpected. The company became more than just employers; they were family to us. By the time I was fourteen, I was working alongside my mother during long summer days, assembling small parts by hand, following the same routine day in and day out. That early experience taught me two things: the value of hard work and the power of dreaming bigger.

My parents, like many others, gave their all with what they had. My dad worked construction from sunrise to sunset, and my mom never shied away from a double shift. They laid the foundation for my resilience, determination, and relentless work ethic. In our household, there was no such thing as giving up.

At night, my sisters and I would gather around the TV to watch *The First 48*. While other kids were watching cartoons, we were imagining ourselves solving crimes. That show ignited a spark in me—a desire to piece together puzzles, uncover the truth, and bring closure to grieving families. Even then, I felt called to protect and serve.

That calling became even more personal with the birth of my son, Israel Natalio. He became my reason and my greatest motivation. Every decision I made from that point forward was driven by my desire to build a better life for him—and to be someone he could look up to.

I began my law enforcement career at just eighteen years old, when I was hired by the Transportation Security Administration (TSA) at O'Hare International Airport, only three months after my birthday. As a transportation security officer, I learned the ropes from the ground up—screening passengers, operating x-ray machines, conducting pat-downs, and ensuring safety protocols were met. It wasn't easy work, but I genuinely enjoyed it.

Then, on May 6, 2008, I took the Oath of Enlistment at the Military Entrance Processing Station (MEPS). I knew I was stepping into something much bigger than myself. I joined the 933rd Military Police Company under the 404th Maneuver

Enhancement Brigade, where I completed six grueling months of military police training. From live grenades and weapons handling to crime scene documentation and tactical interviews, I was being molded into a protector—stronger, sharper, and more committed than ever.

All the while, I was juggling my studies at DeVry University and continuing to work for TSA. There were many, what felt like, never ending days, starting at school as a full-time student, followed by my commute to begin my eight-hour shift with TSA, and ending with an hour and a half train ride to get home. My dedication and determination were instilled in me by both of my parents. Eventually, I joined the Security Transportation Instructors team, helping train the next generation of officers after completing the TSA Instructor Academy.

In 2014, I stepped into a leadership role as a lead transportation security officer, managing a team of fifteen on a checkpoint at one of the busiest airports. But deep down, I felt the pull toward something greater.

What felt like a lifetime ago flew by in the blink of an eye. Seven years later, I continued my law enforcement career with a different agency. That next chapter began on September 21, 2014, when I joined the US Customs and Border Protection (CBP) as a Customs and Border Protection officer (CBPO). After intensive training at the Federal Law Enforcement Training Center in Georgia, I was ready to serve on the front lines. Since then, I've served in multiple specialized units, grown both professionally and personally, and found deep fulfillment in this path.

Throughout my journey, my family has been my backbone. My oldest sister often reminds me how she looks up to me, while my little sister admires my determination. Their kind words have shown me the impact I've had on them. My thirteen-year-old nephew is even following in my footsteps through the Explorer Program, and I now mentor him—not just as his aunt, but as one of his advisors. At the heart of everything is Israel. He has seen my sacrifices, endured my long absences, and grown strong relationships through the love and support of his grandparents. He is my why—my greatest joy and my constant reminder of what truly matters.

God has placed incredible people in my life—friends who became family. Weekly calls, shared milestones, and annual vacations have kept me grounded. One of them, now my son's godfather, entered my life early in my TSA career. Another, a fellow Latina in law enforcement, challenged me to shift my mindset around finances and legacy building. She's the reason I'm sharing my story today—because I hope to pass that light on to others who are ready to receive it.

As Latina women, we must lift each other up. While I've faced moments of isolation and judgment, I've also been blessed with mentors who saw my potential. We, as Latina women, must be each other's mentors. We must hold hands as we walk this path together. We must share our stories, celebrate our wins, and rise together.

One of my biggest turning points came when I realized I needed help. My son's heartfelt words, the concern of my family and childhood best friend, and an ambulance ride to the ER led me to seek therapy.

I'll have to take you back in time about thirteen years ago, when I experienced a traumatic life changing event. I kept this dark secret deep within myself, trying to push the pain further and further down inside me, so it wouldn't be exposed. I hid my secret by keeping myself busy, volunteering for opportunities that required me to leave home, and simply staying distracted. My tactics worked great, at least till COVID-19 was introduced to the world and everything slowly came to a pause.

As the world became confined to their homes, I was no different. Working in law enforcement and being a single mother, I was accustomed to always being on the move. During this period of uncertainty, my dark secret started rising to the surface. As much as I tried, I could no longer keep it under control. I turned to alcohol, taking late night trips to purchase more, always being angry and taking it out on my family and on rare occasions on my son. It took my son asking me, "Mom, are you mad with me? Why do you always look angry?" My son called me out, I had no choice but to do some reflecting. Pretending everything was okay was no longer possible. I had to come face to face with my demons that I avoided for so many years. I thank God for showing me the way and seeking out different avenues for help. Throughout this entire journey I have learned to always put my family before anything. Now I find myself wanting to stay home.

That decision changed everything. Therapy helped me to heal, to grow, and to rediscover my strength. You don't have to have it all figured out to take the first step. Sometimes a piece comes one piece at a time. I'm no longer ashamed to say I needed help—because asking for it made me a better mother, officer, and woman.

I knew that my success was not just my own; it was a testament to the resilience and potential of my community.

A MOMENT OF IMPACT IN LAW ENFORCEMENT

Being a Latina in law enforcement—backed by military service and the ability to communicate fluently in two languages—has empowered me to break barriers I never thought possible. Yet, stepping into this male-dominated field comes with challenges that demand more than just hard work. As women, we're expected to constantly prove our competence, speak with precision, and stand unwavering in our authority. Being in this career field I have learned how to be direct and gain the respect of my peers and superiors. It has taught me not to take things personally.

I have faced cultural biases firsthand, from men of other cultures who do not believe women belong outside the home. For instance, there was an elderly male traveler that refused to interact with me simply because I was a woman in a uniform. He chose instead to only engage in conversation with my male CBPO colleague. Moments like that have only fueled my determination. They've taught me resilience, reinforced my voice, and reminded me that my presence in this space matters. I carry not only my badge and rank, but also the pride of my culture, my community, and every woman who dares to lead in spaces not built for us.

BIOGRAPHY

Guadalupe Jasso has exemplified unwavering dedication to her country through eighteen years of distinguished service with the Department of Homeland Security and the US Armed Forces. From 2008 to 2020, she answered the call of duty and deployed to Afghanistan as a military police officer. She also has spent five impactful years as a criminal intelligence analyst for the Counterdrug Task Force. Guadalupe's commitment to national security continues today in the US Air Force, where she supports critical missions that safeguard communities across the nation.

Through Guadalupe's dedication, determination, and sacrifices throughout her career, she has been honorably recognized for her efforts. She has earned an Afghanistan Campaign Medal, Army Commendation Medal, Army Achievement Medal, National Defense Service Medal, and a Global War on Terrorism Service Medal, just to name a few.

Guadalupe holds several collateral positions, such as a CBP national recruiter, a member of the Honor Guard Program with CBP and while in the Army. She is an advisor for the CBP Explorer Program, CBP financial coach, her Units' career advisor, and supported the bomb detection officers.

As a natural leader, Guadalupe is passionate about spreading her knowledge, providing resources to help individuals succeed. She has built a solid foundation and will continue to provide that guidance to those in need. Guadalupe's goal is to help others to put the pieces of their puzzle together.

Guadalupe's devotion extends beyond the battlefield—she is a proud mother to her son, Israel Natalio, and cherishes their adventures around the world and time spent with loved ones at their campsite. Driven by a powerful sense of purpose, she is building generational wealth and laying the foundation for a legacy that will uplift and inspire future generations.

Guadalupe Jasso
lupitaj8833@gmail.com
LinkedIn: Guadalupe Jasso

Ascending Through the Ranks: A Latina Story of Resilience and Empowerment

LOURDES NAVARRO

"The experience was transformative. I discovered a resilience that I didn't know I possessed."

The biting Chicago wind whipped around me as I stood on the parade route, the crisp notes of a mariachi band cutting through the air. It was the annual Mexican Independence Day Parade in the city's Little Village neighborhood, a vibrant celebration of heritage and community. I was a teenager in the Chicago Police Explorers Program, a vocational American program that allows youth to explore a career in law enforcement. As I was marching alongside my brother, Agustine, I felt a swell of pride. An elderly woman's voice, raspy with age and emotion, pierced through the music. "*¡Que vivan nuestros futuros!*" Long live our future! The words resonated deep within me, planting a seed of purpose that would blossom in the years to come.

Growing up in a close-knit Mexican American household in the 1980s and 1990s, I was instilled with the values of hard work, respect, and loyalty. My parents, immigrants from Mexico who had sacrificed everything for their children's future, were living examples of dedication and perseverance. While they encouraged me to succeed academically and professionally, the concept of a career, especially in a male-dominated field like law enforcement, was foreign to them. There were no female role models in law enforcement in my immediate circle, no visible pathways to guide my ambition.

The lack of representation was a constant hum in the background of my aspirations. I saw the news, the skewed portrayals of my *comunidad*, the systemic inequalities that plagued our neighborhoods. The desire to challenge those narratives, to be a force for positive change, gnawed at me.

College brought a new set of challenges. Undecided on a major, I felt adrift, unsure of my capabilities and direction. The internet was still in its infancy, limiting my access to information and opportunities. Then came the call from an army recruiter, an unexpected invitation to explore a path I had only vaguely considered.

The recruiter, a military police sergeant, painted a picture of service, discipline, and the chance to make a real difference. I was intrigued. The idea of law enforcement as a career was becoming more appealing, but I was also hesitant. A six-year to eight-year commitment was daunting, a life-altering decision that I didn't take lightly.

During this time, I learned that my dad was recently laid off from his job at a manufacturing company in the Chicagoland area. After a week of careful consideration, weighing my fears against my aspirations, I made the decision. I enlisted in the Army Reserves, choosing Military Police as my specialty. It was a step into the unknown, a departure from the familiar comfort of my family and community. But it was also a step towards empowerment, a chance to prove to myself and to others of my capabilities.

Basic Combat Training at Fort Leonard Wood, Missouri, was a crucible. The harsh winter, the rigorous physical demands, the constant pressure—it tested my limits in ways that I never imagined. Yet, I persevered, drawing strength from the values instilled by my parents and the camaraderie I found with my fellow soldiers. I excelled in marksmanship, learned tactical maneuvers, and pushed myself through obstacle courses that challenged my fear of heights.

The experience was transformative. I discovered a resilience that I didn't know I possessed. I learned the importance of teamwork, discipline, and unwavering commitment to a cause greater than myself. I also realized that law enforcement wasn't just a job; it was a calling, a way to serve my community and protect the vulnerable.

A few months after returning from training, the world changed on September 11, 2001. My unit was activated, thrusting us into a new reality of heightened security and global conflict. The deployment was sudden, disruptive, and filled with uncertainty. Leaving my family was difficult, especially for my mother, who worried constantly about my safety. But I knew that this was my duty, my chance to put my training into action.

Serving as a Latina in law enforcement brought unique challenges and opportunities. I quickly realized that I was often the only woman, and the only person of color, in the room. I felt the weight of expectations, the subtle scrutiny that came with being a minority in a predominantly male, white environment. There were moments of doubt, times when I questioned my abilities, and wondered if I truly belonged.

I refused to be discouraged. I used my experiences to connect with the Latino community, building trust and bridging cultural gaps. I spoke Spanish fluently, a valuable asset that allowed me to communicate directly with Spanish-speaking residents, understand their concerns, and provide them with the support they needed.

I became a mentor to younger officers, particularly Latinas, sharing my experiences and offering guidance on navigating the complexities of the job. I understood the importance of representation, of having someone who looked like you, who understood your background, and who could advocate for your success.

Over the years, I rose through the ranks, earning the respect of my peers and superiors. I excelled in specialized training, mastering tactics, firearms, and crisis intervention techniques. I traveled the world, to countries such as Kuwait, and Iraq, and Afghanistan, participating in joint operations and learning from law enforcement professionals from different agencies.

With each achievement, I remained grounded in my values, remembering the elderly woman's words at the parade, the faces of the people I served, and the sacrifices my parents had made. I knew that my success was not just my own; it was a testament to the resilience and potential of my community.

One day, a young Latina officer approached me, her eyes filled with uncertainty. "I don't know if I can do this," she confessed. "It's so hard, being a woman in this field, especially a Latina. Sometimes I feel like I don't belong."

I smiled, recognizing the doubt in the young woman's voice. "I know how you feel," I said. "I felt the same way when I first started. But you are strong, you are capable, and you do belong here. Don't let anyone tell you otherwise."

I shared my own story, the challenges I had to overcome, the lessons I had learned. I emphasized the importance of self-belief, perseverance, and the power of mentorship. I said, "We need you here. We need your perspective, your compassion, and your commitment to justice. You can make a difference, not just for yourself, but for all the young Latinas who will come after you."

Inspired by my words, the young officer straightened her shoulders, a newfound determination in her eyes. "I can do this," she said. "I will do this with resilience and tenacity."

With the support of my mentors, I knew of the importance of paying it forward. Throughout my career, I would be approached by co-workers and friends, both men and women, from all backgrounds who would seek my advice. I am proud of the opportunities to have been able to mentor others from around the world.

At the end of one of the most challenging periods in my law enforcement military career, I realized it was the end of my enlistment contract. I contemplated not re-enlisting, considered taking a break from this career. However, when my unit and I returned home safely, I was overwhelmed with a wave of gratitude. As I stepped off the plane back in the United States, the unit administrator greeted me at the door with an unexpected offer: a promotion to sergeant first class. I was shocked and speechless. Since the beginning of my career, I had never imagined achieving such a rank.

Accepting the promotion came with the requirement to re-enlist for at least three more years, and I wholeheartedly embraced that challenge. I have now proudly served twenty-four years in the military, continually seeking to challenge myself and take on demanding assignments. Each obstacle I faced has shaped me into a more competent individual and professional.

Two years later, I took a bold step and volunteered to attend the US Army Drill Sergeant School. There, I encountered skepticism from some of my peers who doubted my capability, given my soft-spoken nature. Nevertheless, I faced the challenges head-on—early mornings, late nights of studying, and demanding obstacle courses. I persevered and graduated, serving for three years as a senior drill sergeant until I was promoted out of that position.

This journey has taught me that resilience and self-belief are powerful agents for growth. I continue to strive for excellence, embracing every opportunity to grow and inspire others along the way. Each experience has reinforced my commitment to not only overcome challenges but also to uplift those around me, proving that with laser-focus and determination, anything is possible.

As I continue my career, I remain dedicated to co-creating a more just and equitable law enforcement system, one where every officer felt valued, respected, and empowered to serve their community with integrity and compassion. As I rose through the ranks, I carry with me the words of the elderly woman at the parade, "Long live our future!"—a future where all Latinas, and all people, could reach their full potential, free from any barriers.

A MOMENT OF IMPACT IN LAW ENFORCEMENT

One of my most memorable moments during a challenging period in my military law enforcement career was when I was assigned overseas as a supervisor to an all-male team as a sergeant of the guard. During that time, I often grappled with imposter syndrome, feeling like I wasn't truly qualified for my role. Yet, even as the only female, I found a profound sense of camaraderie among my colleagues. There were times when I felt homesick. As a distraction, I maintained a strict fitness routine to stay healthy but also found different ways to socialize with my group.

However, I did encounter adversity; some of my male counterparts sought to challenge my leadership. In moments of doubt, I questioned how I had made it this far in my career. In response, I took the time to self-evaluate my leadership skills and confront those doubts. I reached out to my immediate supervisor, a person I deeply respected, and asked if he had any concerns about my work ethic or leadership style. His reassuring response—that he had no issues with my leadership and that I was successfully accomplishing the mission—filled me with renewed determination and resilience. From that moment on, I vowed to show grit in the face of adversity.

BIOGRAPHY

Lourdes Navarro is a first-generation, bilingual, Mexican American born and raised in the area of Little Village in Chicago. She grew up in a faith-driven household that valued hard work and perseverance. Inspired by her parents' love and dedication, she pursued education and athletics, excelling in basketball, track, and cross-country in high school and college. She is an alum of Chicago State University with her bachelor of science in political science. Her passion for running 5K races to full marathons instilled discipline and mental toughness, shaping her career and future.

After joining the Army Reserves during college, Lourdes found her calling in law enforcement full-time at the age of twenty-seven, she was sworn in as a Customs and Border Protection officer and is stationed at the Port of Chicago. Driven by her core values, she has proudly served to protect the nation for the past twenty-four years in the US Army Reserves and the past seventeen years as a federal officer. She has embodied resilience, service, and commitment to safety such as a military police, drill sergeant, and observer controller trainer. Lourdes is currently serving in a temporary duty assignment at the southwest part of the United States, as a Customs and Border Protection officer.

In 2014, Lourdes attended the US Drill Sergeant School and was awarded the highest score in the Army Physical Fitness test in her class. She received the Iron Drill Sergeant Award prior to her promotion in 2016 to master sergeant.

Lourdes Navarro
Lourdes_navarro2233@yahoo.com
IG: Lyeli1

Guardians with a Purpose

JEANETTE IRMA RAMOS

"You need to make changes to see changes."

I started out working the front desk at a police department, not really thinking it would lead to anything more. My job was straightforward; but over time, I got more involved. I started reading officers reports, learning about laws, and figuring out how to handle situations better on my own. I was actively helping and becoming part of the process. That's when I realized that the job was more than just paperwork and phone calls. I had found something I truly wanted to be a part of. I didn't realize how much I would enjoy it. Every day was different and that's what I liked the most. One moment, I would be gathering details for a report for the officer and the next, I'd be helping someone in distress. What started as a simple desk job became something I was truly passionate about; I knew I wanted to be more than just the first point of contact. I wanted to be out there making a difference.

After nine long years, I finally got hired as a police officer. The moment I had been waiting for finally came. I was proud of myself for never giving up, regardless of how many obstacles I faced along the way. There were times when it felt impossible, but I kept pushing, kept learning, and refused to quit.

My oldest brother, who is a police officer, inspired me; I've always looked up to him. Despite everything he went through, he never gave up. Hearing his stories and seeing his dedication motivated me even more to chase my own dream of becoming a police officer. When I got hired, my brother congratulated me and said he was very proud of me and that meant a lot. He had given me a hard time here and there, but I used it as motivation to prove myself. My parents and sisters were just as proud, but the best part was becoming the first female in my family to become a police officer. It was an amazing feeling.

Both my parents were very supportive but something my daughter once said really stuck with me. She told me, "Mommy, I'm proud of you, but I'm afraid something will happen to you." Her words hit me hard, and it reminded me of the risks that come with this job. More than anything, I wanted to show her the importance of bravery and chasing your dreams, no matter the challenges.

It can get difficult being a single mother and hard for my daughter when I miss birthdays and holidays. This job doesn't just affect me, it affects both of us. I hate missing those moments and I know it hurts her, but I hope she understands that everything I do is for us. More than anything, I want her to know how much I love her and that one day, she'll be proud of me.

As a Latina woman pursuing a career in law enforcement, I faced the challenge of overcoming stereotypes and biases that questioned my abilities. Many people doubted whether I could handle the tough, high-pressure situations of the job simply because of my gender and background. On top of that, balancing cultural expectations from my family with the demanding nature of the job was difficult. It often felt like I had to prove myself in ways others did not. After everything I've been through, I realized that being a Latina, and especially a woman in this field, is not easy. You constantly feel like you have to prove to everyone that you are capable, that you belong, and that you are just as strong and competent as anyone else. Despite these challenges, I stayed focused, determined to break through those barriers, and show that I am more than capable of thriving in this career.

I remember my first few months in the field training program, I faced challenges with one of my field training officers, who doubted my abilities and requested for me to get an extension. I often questioned whether his expectations were higher because I was a woman or if he simply believed I wasn't cut out for the job. Despite the challenges, I refused to let doubt or pressure define me. I stayed focused and worked harder. I put in the work and proved that I was capable of achieving anything.

Throughout my career in law enforcement, I've handled countless difficult calls involving violence and distressing situations. The hardest challenging part is learning how to handle it all without letting it weigh on you mentally and emotionally.

The community I serve is predominantly Hispanic, and I'm frequently called to translate. Being bilingual allows me to bridge the language gap and making sure people fully understand the situation and get the help they need. Unfortunately, when there's a language barrier, some officers may struggle to communicate, which can limit how much assistance they can provide. By stepping in, I ensure that these individuals feel heard, understood, and supported. It's not just about answering calls it's about making sure a scared mother who only speaks Spanish feels safe, or reassuring a young Latina that she's not alone. Being able to bridge that gap and help my community in a way that others might not be able to is what makes this job meaningful to me.

Being a Latina in law enforcement has definitely been an advantage. I can connect with the Hispanic community in a way that not everyone can, especially when language or cultural differences come into play. Speaking Spanish has helped me communicate with people who might otherwise struggle to express themselves, and that goes a long way in building trust. Many people feel more comfortable opening up to an officer who understands their culture, especially in sensitive situations like domestic violence or immigration concerns. It's a great feeling when I respond to a call and hear someone say, *"Ah, que bueno que hablas español mija, Tú sí me puedes ayudar."* I can see the relief on their face, knowing that someone understands them.

When I hit the streets, I'm not just a cop in a uniform. I can be myself, someone who speaks their language and gets what they're going through. For me, it's not always about taking action or enforcing rules it's about making a real impact. Sometimes, it's about listening, showing you care, and being there when people need someone to talk to. It's not just about what I do, but how I make them feel.

I was assigned to a grammar school, and I enjoyed it very much. Spending time with kids and checking on them allowed me to build positive relationships with them and be a role model. It's important for children to see friendly and approachable officers because it helps create trust, makes them feel safe, and teaches them that law enforcement is there to support and protect them. When I was a kid I remember hearing, "If you misbehave, the police will come take you," and for some, that fear felt real. But building trust and real connections can show them that officers are here to help and support their communities. Experiences like these not only strengthen the bond between officers and the community but also shape how young children view law enforcement as they grow up. You need to make changes to see changes.

I've never regretted choosing this career. There are days that can be exhausting and stressful, but I know I made the right decision. The challenges are just part of the job and helping others make a difference and constantly growing makes it all worth it.

I remember one time when I responded to a missing juvenile call. The mother was frantic, worried for her daughter who had been struggling with thoughts of self-harm. She was doing everything she could, but her situation was tough. She had to work multiple jobs but wanted to be there for her kids.

After a lot of searching and worry, the daughter called back. When she came home, she was upset, but I made sure to give her space to talk. Before I left, I gave her my work number and told her she could call anytime whether she needed advice, someone to listen, or just to talk. Later that evening my phone rang, it was her. This time, she really opened up. She told me everything she'd been struggling with, all the things that had been weighing her down. I reminded her not to let bad influences take her off track and that she was so much stronger than she realized. We had an honest conversation, and I offered support. It felt good to help because I knew exactly where she was coming from. You never know how much of an impact simply listening can have. This young girl was struggling with thoughts of self-harm and I truly believe that my ability to connect with her made a difference. The mother in me came out, and I genuinely wanted to get this teenage girl the help she needed.

I think that when young Latinas see someone like them in law enforcement, they feel more comfortable opening up. There's a level of trust and familiarity that makes difficult conversations a little easier. My hope is that as more Latina women step into these roles, young girls will not only feel supported but will also start to see themselves in this profession. If even one of them is inspired to become an officer one day because of that connection, then that, to me, is a success.

Once, I was called to respond to a twelve-year-old girl, who was having a mental health episode. Her grandmother, unable to handle the situation, reached out for help. When I arrived, the girl was acting hysterically, and it was difficult to get her attention at first. But I didn't let it frustrate me. I approached her calmly, trying to understand her feelings and asking what was bothering her. After a few minutes of conversation, I was able to connect with her and to build some rapport. Slowly, she began to trust me.

Eventually, when it was time for her to go to the hospital, she asked if I could ride with her in the ambulance. It meant a lot to me because it showed that she felt comforted and cared for. I reassured her, showing empathy as a mother would. I wanted her to feel safe, knowing she wasn't alone in that moment.

While some men may underestimate women in law enforcement, situations like these show that women can often be more effective because they have the ability to build trust and connect with others. Seeing Latinas in law enforcement sends a powerful message to young people in our community. It shows that we can be leaders, change-makers, and agents of positive transformation. Representation matters, and when Latinas are part of the force, we inspire others to see themselves in these roles and pursue careers where they might have once felt excluded.

In the end, it's not just about enforcement. It's about connecting, listening, and making a difference in ways that go beyond the badge. Having Latinas in law enforcement helps create a more inclusive, understanding, and effective approach to serving diverse communities. Having Latina mentors in the field is incredibly important because they offer guidance and support that is rooted in shared experiences, cultural understanding, and empathy. For many young Latinas or those from similar backgrounds, having a mentor who truly understands their struggles can be a game changer. Latina mentors can provide valuable insight that might be unique to the experience of being a minority in a field like law enforcement. To all the young Latinas, never doubt yourself you are powerful and capable of achieving everything you set your mind to. You come from a legacy of strength and culture, and the world is yours to conquer. So, keep pushing and always believe you can. *¡Sí se puede!*

For the Latina women out there considering a career in law enforcement don't ever think that just because it's a male-dominated field, you can't do it. Female officers matter just as much and bring some strengths to the job that male officers sometimes can't. The process can be tough with the tests, the exams, and the academy, but it's all worth it in the end. It just takes time, dedication, and preparation. Stay focused, put in the work, and don't let anyone discourage you. It's a challenging but incredibly rewarding career. If it's something you truly want, go for it!

A MOMENT OF IMPACT IN LAW ENFORCEMENT

Some moments in life are the ones that make you stop and reflect, realizing how much you've grown. Over the years, you gain experience, learn valuable lessons, and become better because of it. As a police officer, you go from being just another person to someone who can truly make a difference and, sometimes, even a hero in someone's eyes.

Hearing people express their appreciation for what we do means a lot. Of course, not everyone will feel that way, and that's okay. You can't change every opinion, and not everyone will like you. But for those who do see the value in our work, I am happy to help and support them. Just knowing that doing your job sometimes going the extra mile can make a real difference, even shifting someone's perspective on law enforcement, is incredibly rewarding.

BIOGRAPHY

Jeanette Irma Ramos is a dedicated police officer. She pursued her studies in criminal justice at Morton College in Cicero, Illinois. Her commitment to both her family and her career exemplifies her dedication and professionalism.

Jeanette grew up in a Spanish-speaking household with her parents, who immigrated to the United States from Mexico in search of a better environment to raise their family. This background has shaped her perspective and commitment to serving her community.

She is passionate about empowering young Latinas to achieve success and encouraging them to never give up on their dreams. She is thrilled to have recently joined Latinas in Law Enforcement, where she can support young Latinas in their journey. This opportunity allows her to make an even bigger difference in their lives.

Jeanette Irma Ramos
Janetramos1005@gmail.com

A Setback to Success

CLARIBEL RIVERA

"Doubt and setbacks are inevitable, but they should fuel your determination rather than deter you."

I was born and raised in Chicago. I am the oldest of three and grew up on the Northwest Side of the city in the Belmont Cragin neighborhood. I was raised by strong, independent women—my grandmother, my mother, and my three aunts. I am third-generation Mexican American, and my family is from a small village in Guerrero, Mexico. I come from a closely knit family. The unwavering love and support of my mother, grandmother, and aunts shaped me profoundly. Their guidance was instrumental in my life, even in the absence of a father figure.

Their influence has been immeasurable. Without them, I wouldn't be where I am in my career.

At a very young age, I remember constantly visiting my aunt in the hospital, but never really understood the severity of it. I later understood that one of my three aunts was involved in a terrible shooting that left her paralyzed. It was incredibly tough on our family. Seeing my aunt go through that, seeing how vulnerable one can be, really made me think about the importance of having a supportive system and how vital it is to help people find the justice they deserve. This was one of the main reasons that led me to choose my career path.

My entire life I grew up around my aunt and witnessed her struggles. I can only imagine how challenging this was for my grandmother, who only speaks Spanish. My mom and other aunts were fairly young and not well versed with how law enforcement worked. Which made it difficult for them to find justice and have the guidance that they needed at the time.

This made me think of the limited resources available for the Hispanic community at the time and if, indeed, everything was handled the right way. Having that in mind, I knew I wanted to make a difference and help others find safety and justice.

Great opportunities and experiences happened during my last two years of high school. I was introduced to the Chicago Police and Firefighter Training Academy (CPFTA) during my junior year as an after-school curricular activity. This program provided academic credits, as well as an introduction to the field. Without a doubt, this captured my attention instantly and I knew

I wanted to be part of it. This initial exposure fostered my passion for the field. I enjoyed the hands-on activities and experiences that the program had to offer. They structured the program, so that as a cadet you get to experience from both the fire and police side. You create bonds with students from all over the city with different backgrounds, as well as with the instructors, who actively serve or have served in the field.

This program then introduced me to the US Customs and Border Protection Program (CBP), also during my junior year. This program provided a more in-depth insight into law enforcement and a contribution to the community. What I greatly appreciate about this program is that the advisors get to know you on a more personal level; they guide you and mentor you even after high school. The advisors in this program really put in a lot of their time and effort in helping the youth become successful in any field. The program is not just about accountability; it fosters a genuine sense of ownership and empowers participants to develop strong leadership skills. The program's structured approach guides individuals through a journey of self-discovery and personal growth, nurturing the qualities necessary to become responsible and contributing members of society.

Through practical exercises, collaborative projects, and mentorship opportunities, participants gain valuable experience in decision-making, conflict resolution, and effective communication—all essential components of becoming a responsible adult. The program encouraged me step outside of my comfort zone, embrace challenges, and ultimately become confident and capable leaders. These experiences opened doors to opportunities that shaped and solidified my career trajectory in law enforcement.

While my heart was set on a career in law enforcement after high school, I was too young to pursue it at the time. My family initially expressed concerns about the inherent dangers of the profession. However, their unwavering support empowered me to pursue my goals, even if they had reservations. My family was present during fundraisers, community events, competitions, and gave me words of encouragement. I knew I needed to gain experience and build a strong foundation, so I chose to work in security and loss prevention. This role, secured through the connections I made in the youth programs, proved to be a valuable steppingstone. It allowed me to develop skills and build relationships that would serve me well in the future.

Initially, the security work somewhat overshadowed my law enforcement aspirations. However, I eventually realized that completing my education was essential to achieving my long-term career goals. Although my academic journey took longer than anticipated, perseverance taught me the importance of dedication and achieving goals at my own pace. I initially went to school full-time and worked part-time. I then began to work full-time and attended school part-time for roughly six years. I took online classes, sometimes one class per semester which prolonged me completing school. The time spent in my security job also allowed me to mature and gain valuable real-world experience. At the time I felt like I could not reach my objective quick enough and felt a bit discouraged because of my set back, but I ultimately pulled through it. The journey, while challenging, has been incredibly rewarding, and I am immensely grateful for the support and guidance I've received along the way.

My path to becoming a law enforcement officer was anything but linear; it was more like navigating a winding mountain road. For years, I persevered through numerous setbacks, a journey punctuated by periods of self-doubt that led me to temporarily re-evaluate my aspirations. The decision to return to my pursuit, however, proved pivotal. Following a period of challenges, in early 2022, I was fortunate enough to receive a job offer with a law enforcement agency. This opportunity represented a significant turning point, allowing me to leverage my skills and experience in a new environment. While I had previously encountered obstacles, this offer marked a renewed sense of purpose and a chance to contribute.

The academy presented its own unique set of challenges, testing my resilience in ways I never anticipated. Academically, I struggled. I've never been a strong test-taker, and the textbook work felt particularly arduous. Week after week, I found myself among the last two cadets to complete exams, a stark contrast to the many who finished quickly and readily discussed their answers. This fueled my anxieties; the fear of failure loomed large. While I understood that everyone learns at their own pace, the pressure to improve was immense, and the weekly tests felt like a constant uphill battle.

The looming final state exam amplified these anxieties. The thought of disappointing myself and my family weighed heavily on me. The memory of being one of the last two cadets to leave the exam room, among over a hundred, remains vivid. The agonizing wait for results, the uncertainty of success, was perhaps the most difficult aspect of the entire process. The relief of eventually passing was immense, but the fear of failure had left an indelible mark.

Beyond the academic hurdles, the emotional toll was significant. The academy required a geographical relocation, forcing me to separate from my close-knit Hispanic family. This distance was particularly challenging, as family is central to my life, and it meant missing countless cherished moments and making considerable sacrifices. The journey was demanding, both intellectually and emotionally, but ultimately, the reward of achieving my goal made it all worthwhile.

Being a Latina woman in this field has been quite the ride! It's been amazing in so many ways, but there have been some bumps along the road. It wasn't just about dealing with prejudice; it was constantly having to prove myself. A lot of little things, like people misinterpreting my accent or just not taking me seriously because of how I look, or even doubting my physical strength, forced me to work extra hard to show I was more than capable. I had to be really on top of my game. I often felt the need to demonstrate exceptional competence to overcome implicit biases and prove my worth within a male-dominated field.

During my field training, I encountered discouraging words from a colleague who doubted my ability to succeed. This negativity, while painful, ultimately served as a powerful motivator. It solidified my resolve and spurred me to prove them wrong. Throughout my career, I've faced numerous obstacles, but I've consistently found the strength to persevere.

My bicultural background has proven invaluable. As a Latina deputy, I find I can connect with members of the Latino community who may be hesitant to interact with law enforcement due to language barriers or cultural misunderstandings. This ability to bridge communication gaps has been incredibly rewarding.

Three years later, since being hired in 2022, I'm still serving with the same department, a testament to my resilience and dedication. I'm proud of my accomplishments and eager to continue growing within the force. My future aspirations include seeking further growth and taking on greater responsibilities. I aspire to become a detective and being involved in undercover stings.

To aspiring Latina law enforcement officers, I offer this advice: seize every opportunity that comes your way, even if it initially seems unappealing. Embrace challenges as learning experiences and use them to build your skills and expand your horizons. Doubt and setbacks are inevitable, but they should fuel your determination rather than deter you. Your perseverance will ultimately pave the way to success. Never let anyone diminish your potential. Your journey may be challenging, but your strength and resilience will carry you through.

A MOMENT OF IMPACT IN LAW ENFORCEMENT

My initial experiences in law enforcement have challenged the Hollywood portrayal of constant high-stakes action. While there are certainly moments of urgency and excitement, the reality is far more nuanced. My time on the force has been relatively short, yet it's already taught me valuable lessons about the limitations of immediate intervention. There are situations where, despite a strong desire to pursue justice, external factors or procedural requirements restrict immediate action.

I recall one early incident where my priority had to be ensuring a victim received appropriate medical attention, even though I felt a strong urge to immediately investigate the circumstances surrounding the incident. A different course of action could have easily led to a less favorable outcome. This experience underscored the importance of prioritizing immediate needs and adhering to established protocols.

BIOGRAPHY

Claribel Rivera's journey is a testament to the power of family and perseverance. Raised on Chicago's Northwest Side by a strong network of women—her mother, grandmother, and aunts—she learned the value of hard work and dedication from a young age. As the eldest of three siblings, Claribel naturally assumed a leadership role, guiding and supporting her younger brother and sister.

Her path to a career in law enforcement wasn't a predetermined one; in her youth, she lacked clear direction for her future. However, two law enforcement programs during high school and a tragedy to her aunt proved transformative, illuminating a career path she had lost motivation for. This experience, coupled with her academic achievements—including graduation from a Chicago community college and the police academy in Champaign, Illinois—laid the foundation for her current success.

With dedicated service under her belt, Claribel stands at the beginning of a promising and impactful career in law enforcement. Her story inspires many Latinas, highlighting the importance of personal growth and supportive communities in shaping individual destinies.

Claribel Rivera
Crivera_1223@yahoo.com

Inspiration Leads to Inspiration

REBECA RIVERA

"Law enforcement is not just about the badge—it's about stepping up when others step back, about making a difference in your community, and about paving the way for those who will come after you."

When I was thirteen years old, I was traveling back home from Mexico with my family when I had an encounter that would change the course of my life. As we passed through a checkpoint, I was struck by the sight of a Latina woman in uniform, standing confidently at her booth. She wasn't just doing her job; she commanded respect with a quiet authority and professionalism I had never seen before. At that moment, it dawned on me that I had never witnessed a woman in such a role, especially in a field dominated by men. This wasn't just an immigration checkpoint—this was a woman owning her space and her power.

Feeling a mix of awe and curiosity, I boldly approached her and asked how someone like me could learn about this field. She smiled warmly, shared details about the Police Explorer Program, and encouraged me to pursue it. The program provides a training environment for youth ages 13-20 interested in the law enforcement career field, learning fundamental techniques and applying them in national, state, and local competitions. That brief conversation sparked something inside me—an excitement and determination I couldn't ignore. It was the first time I realized that law enforcement was a career path open to women like me, and it ignited a dream that would guide my future. That single moment was the beginning of a journey that would ultimately shape my career as an officer.

I became a Law Enforcement Explorer soon after, and I was a part of the program for five incredible years. It was an experience that changed my life, allowing me to gain hands-on knowledge of the field, learn leadership skills, and make lifelong connections. The Explorer program was where I first truly immersed myself in law enforcement, and it solidified my passion for serving others. During that time, I met my husband—he was also an Explorer in the program. We bonded over our shared dedication to law enforcement and our dreams of one day becoming officers. We supported each other through the challenges, and our partnership grew both professionally and personally. It's no exaggeration to say that the Explorer Program was instrumental in shaping not only my career but also the life I would go on to build with my husband and four children.

However, my path to law enforcement was delayed. When my husband began his career in law enforcement, our children were still young. At that point, I made the decision to step back from my own education and work to focus on raising our children. It wasn't an easy decision, but I wanted to be there for them as they grew, to provide them with the stability and support they needed. I became a stay-at-home mom, fully dedicated to my family. For many years, my focus was on raising my children and ensuring that they had the best possible upbringing.

During those years, I set aside my own dreams, but the idea of pursuing a career in law enforcement never fully left my heart. I knew that when the time was right, I would return to it. It wasn't until I was thirty-four, when my children were older and more independent, that I felt it was the right moment to finally step forward. I was ready to pursue my dream—no longer just for myself, but as an example for my children that it's never too late to chase your goals.

I was never the most physically fit person in the room, and the physical demands of the academy were intimidating. But I trained hard. I pushed myself beyond my comfort zone, knowing I needed to prove not just to others, but to myself, that I could succeed. The physical challenges were real, but the real test was the mental strength to keep going, to fight through self-doubt. Every day I reminded myself that I had already overcome so much as a mother and as a Latina in a world that often underestimated me. If I could raise a family and manage everything life had thrown at me, I could succeed at the academy.

One of the toughest challenges, however, came from someone I deeply admire—my father. My dad has always been the hardest-working person I know. He worked minimum-wage jobs his entire life, but his work ethic was second to none. He taught me the importance of perseverance and grit. However, when I shared my dreams of becoming a police officer, he hesitated. He told me that because I had started my family so young, I would never have a career. He believed I needed to stay at home to care for my children, and that a career in law enforcement wasn't a realistic path for someone in my position. His words stung, especially coming from someone I looked up to. I understood that his views were shaped by cultural norms and his own experiences, but it was still hard to hear.

However, those words also became a driving force for me. I knew that I could break through the barriers set by others. And after I graduated from the academy, my father's opinion of women in law enforcement changed. He came to me and said, "I'm proud of you." His words meant the world to me, because I knew they came from a place of deep respect. My success had shifted his perspective, and that, in turn, gave me a sense of validation that was hard to put into words.

After completing the academy, I was assigned to work in Laredo for a year. It was a bittersweet experience—being away from my family was incredibly difficult, and I often felt guilty for pursuing my dreams while my children were at home without me. But I knew that my work was important, and that I was paving the way for my children and others to see that women, and Latinas in particular, belong in this field.

My husband was an incredible source of support throughout my journey. He believed in me even when I doubted myself. He encouraged me to keep going, especially when the road got tough. Having someone by my side who truly understood my goals and the challenges I faced made all the difference.

During my time in Laredo, my mother played a key role in supporting my dreams. Not only did she help take care of my children while I was away, stepping in when I couldn't be there, but she also became a constant source of inspiration for me. Growing up, I saw how she got married at a young age, and despite the challenges she faced, she never gave up on her own aspirations. Her resilience and determination fueled my own drive to pursue my goals. I'll never be able to express enough gratitude for her willingness to step up and be there for my family so I could focus on my career. It truly takes a village, and my village was filled with love, sacrifice, and the unwavering belief in the importance of following your dreams.

Unfortunately, after a year I had to leave my post in Laredo due to a family emergency—my daughter fell seriously ill, and I needed to be with her. I applied for a hardship request to transfer back home, but it was denied. The decision to leave wasn't hard in the sense that I knew my family needed me, but it was still heartbreaking. I had worked so hard to get to this point, and walking away from a career I was passionate about, not knowing if or when I would be able to return, was devastating. I spent a year away from law enforcement, uncertain about what the future held. While it was clear I had to prioritize my family, the emotional weight of leaving my career behind was something I never expected to feel so deeply.

But as with every challenge, I found a way back. It took a full year for me to get back into law enforcement. I had to prove myself all over again, but I knew I wasn't giving up. I had learned so much in my time away—not just about law enforcement, but about what it truly means to serve, to sacrifice, and to fight for your dreams. Once my daughter felt better, I was able to return to the job I loved, stronger and more determined than ever.

However, just as I was settling back into my role, life threw another curveball. In 2015, my husband suffered a debilitating injury while on duty. He was involved in a training exercise that resulted in a simple fracture—one that, over time, spiraled into a series of complex and serious health complications. What was initially expected to be a minor setback has turned into a ten-year battle with chronic pain, repeated hospital stays, amputations, and ongoing medical treatments.

At the time, our children were still relatively young—in middle school and high school. Suddenly, I found myself not only balancing my career but also taking on the role of caregiver. It was a period of intense stress, as I tried to continue working while caring for my husband and making sure our kids were supported through it all. Juggling these responsibilities was incredibly challenging. But I was determined to keep moving forward. I had learned that life would always present obstacles, but it was up to me how I faced them. Even when things felt impossible, I knew that my family's strength and resilience would carry us through.

Despite these challenges, the Explorer Program remained a cornerstone of my journey. I dedicated myself to mentoring and guiding young people, just as I had been guided when I was an Explorer. I passed on the same values of leadership, service, and resilience that were instilled in me. I was proud to see all four of my children follow in our footsteps, each of them participating in the program and carrying on the legacy of service and dedication to the community as officers themselves. They've taken everything I taught them—about resilience, service, and hard work—and applied it to their own careers.

I'm incredibly proud of them, and my heart swells with pride knowing that they, too, are making a difference in this world. We've always emphasized the importance of giving back to the community, whether through volunteer work, youth engagement, or simply helping those in need. My hope has always been to teach my children that life isn't just about what you can get, but what you can give to others.

To the young Latinas out there considering a career in law enforcement: I see you. I believe in you. And I hope my story encourages you to take that first step toward your own dreams. With resilience, confidence, and belief in yourself, anything is possible. Law enforcement is not just about the badge—it's about stepping up when others step back, about making a difference in your community, and about paving the way for those who will come after you. Don't let anyone tell you it's not your place. Your place is wherever you decide to make it.

A MOMENT OF IMPACT IN LAW ENFORCEMENT

One of the most impactful moments in my law enforcement career came through my involvement with the Law Enforcement Explorer program. Over the years, I had the privilege of mentoring several young individuals eager to pursue careers in law enforcement. Watching them grow from motivated teenagers into dedicated young adults was incredibly rewarding.

While many former Explorers chose to follow in our footsteps and become officers, others pursued different paths—some joined the military, while others chose careers in fields like firefighting or emergency medical services. Regardless of the direction they chose, the Explorer program instilled in them a sense of discipline, responsibility, and service that guided them throughout their journeys.

Seeing these individuals succeed and make a difference in their communities, whether through law enforcement or other public service roles, reinforced the importance of mentorship. It reminded me that the true impact of the Explorer Program isn't just about training future officers; it's about shaping responsible, service-minded individuals who will go on to positively influence and inspire the world around them.

BIOGRAPHY

Rebeca Rivera is a dedicated law enforcement professional with over thirteen years of experience, demonstrating a strong commitment to service, leadership, and community engagement. Raised in a family that emphasized the values of hard work and perseverance, she found her passion for law enforcement at the age of thirteen, inspired by a Latina officer. This inspiration led her to join the Law Enforcement Explorer Program, where she spent five formative years honing her leadership abilities and deepening her dedication to public service.

After taking time off to raise her children, Rivera returned to law enforcement at thirty-four, determined to show her family that it is never too late to pursue one's dreams. Throughout her career, she has successfully balanced the demands of law enforcement with her responsibilities as a mother, wife, and caregiver.

In addition to her work as an officer, Rivera dedicated twelve years as an Explorer advisor, mentoring countless young individuals and imparting the values of resilience, leadership, and service. A proud mother of four officers, she has fostered a family legacy of public service. Rivera believes in the transformative power of perseverance and is passionate about inspiring others to overcome obstacles and pursue their dreams.

Rebeca Rivera
18rebecarivera@gmail.com

Forged in Struggle, Built in Strength

LISSETTE RIVERO

"Women in law enforcement face many challenges working in a male-dominated environment."

B eing the police has always been my destiny. I am a retired police officer and currently a real estate broker in the Chicagoland area. I am the youngest of four siblings, of Puerto Rican descent, born and raised a Bible-thumping Pentecostal. I come from very humble beginnings, within the lower economic bracket, raised by a single mother. Needless to say, life was not easy.

At a very young age, when I looked at my family, I saw my potential future. I was six years old when my seventeen-year-old sister got married and moved out. When my older brother turned seventeen just a year later, he also left by enlisting in the US Marines. I believe this was due to the constant moving and the domestic violence in the house. They escaped the chaos that I would endure for a few more years. I was terrified of being left alone, so whenever my remaining sister threatened to run away, I would beg her not to leave me, too.

As an early teen, I sought what many kids look for in all the wrong places. I had the need to belong by hanging with wannabe gangbangers and learning all I could about gang signs, colors, and which gangs were part of the People Nation and which ones were the Folks. People Nation was an alliance of Chicago street gangs that included gangs like the Latin Kings and Vice Lords. The Folks was an alliance of the street gangs that included the Gangster Disciples, Imperial Gangsters, and the Maniac Latin Disciples.

By the time I got to high school, everything and anything aside from studying interested me. I had horrible grades, mostly due to the lack of structure in my home. No one instilled the importance of education. I was a poor student my entire school-age life. I still have nightmares of how failing out of geometry and being unable to graduate. (Luckily, I did pass and graduate.)

I solved my first crime in my senior year. Believe it or not, I was a cheerleader. I had placed my lettermen's jacket in my locker and must have not secured the padlock. Later that afternoon, I found that my jacket had been stolen. I freaked out. We didn't have much money, and I had been working since my sophomore year to help my mother pay the rent, so losing that jacket broke my heart and pissed me off.

I immediately reported it to security, which consisted of Chicago Police resource officers. Our school needed actual police officers because it was centrally located between two rival gangs, which led to a lot of fights inside and outside of the school. An occasional gun shooting was not unheard of either. As a result, security had bigger fish to fry than to worry about my stolen jacket. So, I set off to find the villain myself.

We had escalators in our high school and every day after class I would head to the first floor as fast as I could to stand at the bottom of the escalators and watch as everyone came down. After a few days, it happened. The moron who stole my jacket was dumb enough to wear it. I knew it was mine because it had a cheer letter and a few other patches. Instead of sewing my patches on, I tried to iron it and burned a small section on the front of the jacket. I also knew exactly where all the other patches had been sewn. So, when I saw my jacket on this kid, I raced over to security, grabbed him by the arm and pulled him to the escalator to point this jacket-stealing thief out. That is how I solved my very first case. I remember that feeling of outsmarting the stupid criminal (well, high school kid who swiped my jacket). I suppose this was the first sign of my future.

After high school, I had no idea what to do with my life. I was more concerned with my love life than planning a future. I was working as a receptionist for a non-profit organization in Chicago when I met an intern named Matt. We hit it off and it wasn't long before we started dating. Matt was different from anyone running in my circles. First, he was white and, second, he was educated and had a plan for his future. We started dating in his junior year of college where he was studying to become a chemical engineer. We spent many days talking about school and his interviews and potential income after college. While we dated, I decided if I was going to be with a smart guy then I needed to be smart, too. So, I enrolled in a junior college.

Shortly after he graduated college with his fancy degree, he broke up with me. I always felt like he left because I wasn't smart enough. I wasn't determined. I had no real plans for a career like he did. Who could blame him? After the dust settled and I straightened my crown, I realized I needed to get my shit together. That was a pivotal point in my life.

I continued with school and got married at the age of twenty-two to my high school sweetheart. With the encouragement of a dear friend, I tested for the local county sheriff's department and was hired as a correctional officer. It wasn't a dream job but for someone with just a high school diploma, I was proud. I soon realized I got married for all the wrong reasons and divorced a year later.

My career in corrections worked out well for me. I found that my knowledge of gangs from my younger years taught me how to deal with the inmates. I worked those tiers tall (I'm only five feet, two inches tall) and proud. I had confidence and demanded respect, which I received even from the most hardened criminals. About six years later, I became a correctional instructor at the training academy. What an accomplishment, I thought. Here is a kid from Humboldt Park, who graduated high school by the skin of her teeth and is now teaching others to be the best correctional officers they could be. I was on top of the world.

I had been an instructor for a few years when my academy director called me into his office and told me I was taking the police exam. He apparently saw something in me I had not seen. Although I was confident in my ability as a correctional officer and academy instructor, I had no confidence that I could make it as a street cop. I took additional college courses to obtain the credits I needed to take the police exam. I passed, made the list, and started the police academy in January 2002. I had remarried while working in corrections and was mother to a little boy and baby girl. I juggled motherhood and the police academy and found it to be quite challenging. Little did I know the real challenges were still to come.

I hit the streets on the midnight shift that spring and by the fall my marriage started to fall apart. My husband was a correctional officer, and I was the police. With the insecurities among other toxic factors, we were doomed. Not only was my marriage failing, but the midnight shifts and the job were kicking my butt.

I remember working midnights with a female sergeant who hated women. I learned that I needed to work that much harder to prove myself and I was not going to let her win. It was my first experience with a female supervisor who reveled in seeing other women fail. From that experience I vowed to help other women in my field succeed. Women in law enforcement face many challenges working in a male-dominated environment. When I started my career as a police officer, there was a disproportionate number of men hired compared to women. Let's face it, most women do not have the physical strength to take down a bigger, stronger adversary, but I worked through many aspects of law enforcement that required a female police officer. In recent years, there has been a significant increase in the number of women hired and that's amazing.

Due to the lack of covert women police officers, I was transferred to the Special Operations Unit in 2006. Our unit investigated crimes involving human-trafficking, child exploitation, prostitution, fencing operations, and organized crime, in general. I worked undercover for about nine years. Much of my undercover work involved prostitution. I was a decoy; and in my most run-down clothes and messed up hair, I pretended to be a prostitute, and Johns (aka solicitors of prostitution) were arrested. These stings were either conducted in the early morning hours or at night on the street corner or in hotel rooms where we were a little more upscale. We often conducted these stings in collaboration with other smaller police departments that did not have female undercover officers. In other words, I was a low-paid actress and, frankly, I deserved an Oscar for some of my performances. Those were the days!

Due to the lack of covert women police officers, I had many opportunities to work with various police departments and federal agencies. In 2015, I was detailed to the Federal Bureau of

Investigation (FBI) as a task force officer in the Cyber Crimes Squad. We investigated romance scams, bank fraud, wire fraud—just about anything that involved the internet and fraud. Working with the feds was the biggest honor of my career as those are not afforded to most police officers, let alone a female.

During this time not only was I juggling my demanding job and being a single mother, but I decided to go back to school to get my degree. Although it was not a requirement at this point in my career, I wanted to lead by example so that I could encourage my kids to go to college. I received my bachelor's degree in criminal justice and called it a day. While working with the feds I ran into an old friend from college. A few years later, he became my current husband and my best friend. He (my handsome fireman) is everything I dreamed a husband should be. You know what they say, "Third time's a charm."

After a few years I realized working with the feds wasn't for me. The pace was slower than I was used to and to be honest, once I learned something, I'd move on to the next challenge. So, I transferred back to my department to work in the Criminal Division of the Office of Professional Review. Basically, I investigated dirty cops.

I finally retired in 2019, at the age of fifty with twenty-five years of service. I was content with my career, and I was ready to pass the baton to the younger rookies. Ironically, my last day on the job was my son's first day in the Chicago Police Academy. I am now a proud police mom.

A MOMENT OF IMPACT IN LAW ENFORCEMENT

The most impactful case in my career was in 2006. I was a fairly new covert officer, and a neighboring police department needed assistance with a complaint of a neighborhood doctor accused of sexually assaulting his patients. At the time, I was one of a few Hispanic female undercover officers and I accepted the task. I went undercover as a new patient and concocted a story that would lead the doctor to believe I would never report him to the police. During my first visit, he checked my heart rate by placing his hand inside my shirt and underneath my right breast. By the second visit, my left breast was completely exposed as he took my heart rate. Before there could be a third visit, the office was raided, and the doctor was arrested. After the press conference that weekend, twenty-one women came forward.

When I walked into court for his trial, I looked right at him. Never in my career had I cared more to see a suspect indicted. The best part was knowing that there is no greater service than being the one who made it happen and helped bring justice to the twenty-one victims.

BIOGRAPHY

Lissette Rivero is a retired Police Officer, having served for twenty-five years with the Cook County Sheriff's Police Department. Lissette served in multiple units during her tenure. She began her career as a correctional officer in 1994 and later became a corrections training academy instructor before she was promoted to the Police Department in 2002. She served four years in patrol.

From 2006 to 2015, she was assigned to the Special Operations Unit where she worked as an undercover investigator conducting various criminal investigations involving prostitution, trademark violations, human trafficking, organized crime, theft, and fraud. Many of these cases were in collaboration with other municipalities, including other local police departments, FBI, Secret Service, Homeland Security, Food and Drug Administration, and US Department of Agriculture.

She became a task force officer with the FBI in 2015 conducting investigations on cybercrime and internet scams. In 2017, Lissette continued her career with the Cook County Sheriff's Office of Professional Review where she conducted investigations involving complaints against sheriff's sworn personnel involved in criminal activity. Her collateral duties involved extraditing female detainees from other states and was a member of the Hostage Barricade Team.

Lissette is now a full-time real estate agent specializing in working with first responders. Lissette is an active member and recording secretary on the Executive Board of the Fraternal Order of Police (FOP) Lodge 4.

She is the wife of a retired firefighter lieutenant and the mother of two adult children, one of which is a Chicago police officer.

Lissette Rivero
lrivero674@yahoo.com

Querer Es Poder

JULIE RODRIGUEZ

"That moment wasn't just about a new job, it was the beginning of stability, opportunity, and generational change."

I grew up on the South Side of Chicago in the humble Hispanic neighborhoods of Pilsen and Little Village—where even the *paleteros* knew our family gossip. My mother, Elisa, and her sisters were inseparable. Immigrating to the Windy City was no exception. When one sister moved into a new neighborhood, everyone else followed. We lived so close together, we didn't need WhatsApp—we'd just open a window and yell.

My mom, a strong Latina, was a single mother to my sister

and I. She came from a family of eleven siblings where everyone had to chip in to make sure there was food and clothing for the family. Education wasn't encouraged and most of my mom's siblings didn't get past primary school. My mother, who loved learning, found herself a job at nine years old. She was the companion and caretaker of another nine-year-old girl, which included accompanying her to school. The family allowed my mother to live with them as long as she kept up with her duties and helped out at the family's multiple stores. That's the Latina hustle, making moves even at nine years old! My mom's strong work ethic carried down to me and I still look up to her.

My sister and I didn't have much, but we also didn't need much—just *frijoles*, *cariño*, and Vicks VapoRub. When we lived on 18th and Racine, I remember the neighborhood kids playing tag and hide-and-seek in abandoned buildings, turning Pilsen's rough edges into our version of Disneyland. Even though Pilsen was rough in the 1980s, I never felt unsafe. Perhaps it was because my world was *pequeño*, tiny enough that everywhere I turned I'd run into a cousin or some other familiar face. In our neighborhood, security wasn't an alarm; it was family.

The happiest home I remember was on the Southwest Side. My aunt Emelia bought a multi-unit building and we all crammed in. It was such a fun place to live because there were so many kids, both in our building and on our block. There was always someone to play with, always something to do, and always some adventure. Our imaginations had no limits, powered by friendship, laughter, and the occasional *chancletazo*, if we got too wild.

It was while living there that my mother met my stepfather, the only father I've known. They were soon married and eventually gave my sister and I three brothers. Their first marital home was a small house nearby on Whipple Avenue. That house became the scene of a few moments that would shape the trajectory of our lives. For a hot minute, my mother was a homemaker but knowing her hustle, that didn't last long. One day, while driving down Kedzie Avenue, something caught her eye—a simple sign advertising real estate classes at a local office. She saw an opportunity and grabbed it faster than *pan dulce* at breakfast. She signed up on the spot, studied hard, and became a licensed realtor. That moment wasn't just about a new job, it was the beginning of stability, opportunity, and generational change.

Prior to my mom becoming a realtor, adults around me mainly held labor and factory jobs. Now, more than three decades later, my mom is still a successful realtor. She set the bar high, leading by example and inspiring me every step of the way. Through her hard work and determination, she carved a path for my siblings and I, teaching us to dream bigger, reach higher, and to never, ever settle.

Around the same time, a couple of Jehovah's Witness preachers knocked on our door and soon after my mom was deep into Bible studies. She took to the religion and brought us kids along for the ride. Suddenly, Sundays weren't just about going to the mall or *carne asadas;* they were about meetings at the Kingdom Hall. Her newfound faith sparked passion within her but also created a rift within the family. My stepfather wasn't on board, creating a divide that reshaped our family dynamic. I remember having stomach aches when they fought over religion. My siblings also took to the religion but I did not. It wasn't easy, but it taught me about conviction and standing firm. Eventually, when I turned eighteen, I moved out and began my own story. I bounced around between family and friends' homes until I finally got my own place, guided by those lessons of resilience my mom unknowingly passed on.

I met my future husband when I was nineteen years old (now ex-husband, thank goodness). When we had our son Aden, my ex-husband insisted that we work opposite shifts to care for him so I traded my job as an administrative assistant for a night-shift data entry position at the federal government. Unfortunately, my ex-husband was a *machista* and our marriage was a roller coaster of highs and lows. One day when Aden was just a few months old, I saw a look on his face that broke my heart—fear. He was scared listening to his parents argue the same way I'd heard my parents fight years ago. I knew right then that I couldn't repeat the cycle. I had to break free, *por mi hijo,* and to find a life with peace, not echoes of my past.

When my ex and I finally split, the federal agency I was working for began hiring benefit adjudicators. Seeing an opportunity to show Aden that we can always strive for more, I applied and moved up. I later got promoted to be an investigator—opening a door I'd never imagined. It was then that I became exposed to the position of special agent. Before then, special agents only existed in Hollywood for me. However, I came to find out that a special agent is much more than a police officer; they are criminal investigators. I was fascinated by the position. I also wanted to show my son that our roots don't limit our dreams; they fuel them. I was determined. I was going to be a special agent.

I reviewed every special agent posting I could find. I needed to know what it took to become a special agent. I found education to be a common theme. I also felt that, as a Latina, I had to make myself stand out. If a bachelor degree was required, then I would obtain a bachelor and master degrees. I wasted no time in getting registered at the local community college. I ended up earning an associate degree and a bachelor degree in criminal justice, as well as a master degree of public administration.

Taking care of Aden primarily on my own, working full-time, and going to school full-time wasn't easy—but nothing worthwhile ever is. On top of all that, Aden began struggling at school and we began a long, convoluted, and painful journey to find the right special needs services for him. This made me crave stability for him even more. Every career move mattered. Special agents in federal law enforcement come in many flavors; some require relocating across the country while others regularly pull late-night stakeouts. I scoured job listings looking for the perfect fit—a career where I could keep climbing without missing bedtime stories.

Then one day, I received a call from a small federal agency specializing in white-collar investigations. It presented a stable, meaningful position at home in Chicago. It was perfect for me!

The hiring process felt like an endless *novela*—two interviews, medical exams, and a thorough background check—but I made it through. In May 2019, I officially became a special agent. What came next was twelve intense weeks at the Federal Law Enforcement Training Center in Glynco, Georgia, where I learned everything from law to investigative techniques and firearms. During that time, Aden was lovingly cared for by a village of fierce *mujeres:* my mom, my ex-husband's mom, and my cousins Nelly and Mari. They stepped up with love and support, making sure Aden had everything he needed while momma chased her dreams.

Special agent training was rigorous and demanding, and I had doubts, but it was exactly the challenge I needed to continue shaping our family's story for the better. If you've been through any kind of boot camp before, acclimating to special agent training probably feels normal. But for me? *¡Ay Dios mio!* Not at all! Most of the trainees seemed to come from military or law enforcement backgrounds and were used to people shouting orders and making them march around with gear heavier than my *tía's pozole* pot. I was used to chasing a toddler, not jogging half a mile with thirty pounds of equipment in blazing heat. They dictated everything: what to wear, how to get around, where and when to eat, and even how to breathe (okay, not really—but it felt that way!). The schedule was tight; we were constantly struggling to be at the right place, at the right time, and with the correct equipment. It was tough! It challenged even the more experienced trainees. But it was also incredible. We had phenomenal instructors and a unique training center, and some of the stories I heard were straight out of Netflix crime specials.

After training wrapped up, I wasted no time heading back home to Chicago to reunite with Aden and start my new chapter as a special agent. Thankfully, I had motivating jefes who knew how to support a Latina determined to thrive professionally without sacrificing *familia*. My new gig came with predictable hours, perfect for a mom raising a kiddo.

You know those fancy special agents on TV—the ones that whisper into hidden earpieces, kick down doors, and take down criminals with MMA-style moves? *Bueno,* that's definitely not me. I'm more of the nerdy *agente especial* type. My cases involve tracking down fraud when someone messes with government money or programs. Instead of dramatic takedowns, my thrill comes from untangling financial mysteries, tracking down documents, and investigative research. I put on my analyst hat and connect the dots in bank records, emails, etc. There is a lot of power in investigating behind a computer screen. Once I am done, the picture I am able to paint is damning and irrefutable. But don't get me wrong—when it's time, I jump into action, carrying out surveillance, conducting interviews, coordinating raids, and teaming up with US Attorney's offices to bring criminals to justice. It might not make for exciting sitcoms but I wear that nerd badge proudly—keeping an eye on taxpayer dollars like an *abuela* counting change at the *mercado*.

There are plenty of perks to being a special agent— like knowing the work I do has purpose and real impact. My investigations genuinely matter. I also get to team up with some incredible people—special agents, investigative analysts, forensic experts, detectives, *policías*, attorneys, you name it. Everyone brings their own unique story to the table and I'm blessed to call these dedicated folks my colleagues and *amigos*.

There are also downsides to my position. Sometimes I have to travel for cases or to lend a hand to colleagues, and while catching flights sounds glamorous, it can be tough on *familia*. I'm also mindful of the responsibility and power that come with being a special agent. My investigations affect real lives and the consequences can mean prison time, drained bank accounts, or limited career opportunities. It's heavy stuff, so I handle it with care, knowing my decisions can ripple through people's lives. Federal law enforcement also lacks diversity and many times when I walk into a meeting, I am the only Hispanic or only woman, or both. It can be lonely. Perhaps that is why I cling to other cops that look like me. It makes me smile when I see another successful Latina. I know most of us had to claw our way up by making tough life choices.

Despite the weight of it all, I genuinely love what I do. I feel incredibly fortunate to serve in this role, grateful each day that my *mamá* taught me to hustle, stay humble, and handle my responsibilities *con respeto*.

A MOMENT OF IMPACT IN LAW ENFORCEMENT

My son Aden, who is autistic, struggled in school since he began pre-kindergarten at three years old. To our dismay, his needs were regularly ignored and pushed aside. The schools he attended refused to provide the necessary services and therapies for him because it would cost them financially. This injustice was extremely frustrating and disheartening. I had no experience with special needs myself, and as a new mother, I had to learn to advocate and fight for what Aden needed to be successful and independent in life. There had to be a future for kids like Aden.

I didn't know it at the time but this fight for justice gave me the skills I needed to become a successful investigator. My tenacity and relentlessness researching different needs made me an effective fact-finder. When I entered government work and investigations, I was able to use those skills to investigate criminals and protect the community. Although I am mainly behind the scenes working on fraud cases, I help keep people accountable for their wrongdoing. The fight I lead is impactful and has given me purpose.

BIOGRAPHY

Julie Rodriguez was born and raised in Chicago. She is the second eldest of five kids. She attended Chicago Public Schools for her elementary education and attended a suburban high school, where she graduated as a junior. She attended a small secretarial school for what would have been her senior year and then entered the workforce as an assistant in an insurance company.

In 2008, Julie began working for the federal government in various positions until she landed a job as an investigator. It was then that her path was paved to become a special agent. However, Julie had to pursue an undergraduate degree first. She returned to school and obtained an associate degree in criminal justice from Moraine Valley Community College, a bachelor's degree in criminal justice from Roosevelt University, and a master of public administration from the University of Illinois at Springfield.

Julie received the biggest promotion of her career in 2019 when she was hired as a special agent for a federal agency. In her short time as a special agent, she has received numerous awards and recognitions.

Julie truly enjoys her work, which is reflected in her case outcomes. She still lives in Chicago with her son, Aden. She enjoys working out, the outdoors, theater, cooking, DIY, and spending time with loved ones.

Julie Rodriguez
info@latinasinlawenforcement.com

She Believed She Could, So She Did

NINA RODRIGUEZ

"My uniform didn't define me—my integrity, my actions, and my dedication did."

Growing up in the early 1990s was the best time. I grew up in a city full of authenticity. Big cities are full of excitement and diversity. An unknown author stated, "Do you know why sidewalks were created? Cause the streets ain't for everybody!"

My parents made tremendous sacrifices for my brother and me—sacrifices that I now deeply understand as a mother to my gorgeous twins. The tough love and discipline they gave was to help us be productive citizens in our community, which was given with love. My parents worked effortlessly to send my brother and

I to private school. They were traditional Latino parents who exercised communication, structure, and created a foundation for my brother and I to flourish. They taught us morals, values, principles, and respect, which I have instilled in my children. They were our first role models, mentors, and supporters in all we did. They did not tolerate hate or disrespect and spoke when needed. I am who I am because of my upbringing.

I am a proud Puerto Rican Latina, a daughter, sister, mother, wife, cousin, niece, and friend. I am not everyone's cup of tea, and that's okay, I was never meant to be. I don't have to fit the mold; I could redefine it. I am bold, unique, passionate, and I love deeply. I have a passion that vigorously runs through my veins. For the last nineteen years, I have been blessed to exemplify my character and personality through my calling in law enforcement.

I grew up in a large city in the 1990s, captivating summer nights will forever be embedded in my memories. The sirens and colors of police, fire, and ambulances echo in the madness of celebrations, festivals, and city living. This large-scale city came together and took pride in how beautiful it was. Back then, I was a young, fierce, unstoppable *Boricua* who saw the change she wanted to be and knew she had a calling. I didn't fit the traditional image of what a police officer looked like, especially not in a male-dominated field. This only made me more determined.

The pride I have for my Puerto Rican heritage runs deep and stands out in my career. I believed I could—and I did. Growing up I was exposed to gang-infested neighborhoods and crime. In the late 1990s policing was different. I saw the beauty and struggle of tight-knit neighborhoods that were filled with culture and pride, but also the weight of crime, mistrust, and tough realities. The police weren't just a symbol; they were present. Sometimes protective, sometimes feared. My view of law enforcement was shaped early, not just by what I saw, but by what I felt. There was some level of "respect" towards cops and authority. Witnessing police officers' interactions within "certain" communities enticed my calling even further.

As a child I always knew I wanted to pursue the field of military or law enforcement. However, this field is a calling and I carried my past with me. My dream was to show beyond a doubt that Latinas and women in law enforcement can do the same job as men. I felt that I could bring the police and communities together through understanding and commitment. Being raised in a big city, I rarely saw Latina officers. The streets and neighborhoods I once hung out in, I would soon be patrolling. I truly believed that I could set a different approach or direction for the department—a strong Latina who wanted to inspire all females and exhibit that we can take on the career of law enforcement and still stay true to who we are as individuals.

During this pursuit into law enforcement, I had no warning about mental health nor the amount of trauma an officer can experience the entirety of our careers. Still, the very next day, we are lacing our boots, strapping on our vests, and ready to hit the hard, cold, cruel streets. A Latina in law enforcement means overcoming barriers and challenges of a profession that traditionally is dominated by men. Latinas, demonstrate trust building through showing empathy and resilience within all communities.

Policing nowadays has a variety of ethnicities and more females are pursuing this career. Joining the force in 2005, I had no idea what I was embarking into, but I was driven by purpose. My uniform doesn't define me—my integrity, my actions, and my dedication do. The moment I put on that uniform I realized just how deep stereotypes ran. Views on women in policing from society can quickly diminish your goals and ambitions if you allow it. You may be labeled by others as weak for showing emotion or empathy. You will deal with "outside" trauma, but also department trauma. Some fellow officers will create hell for you because of who you are. I was overlooked, underestimated, and dismissed because I was a woman. There have been times where I would speak and not be acknowledged for my conversation. My work ethic is strong but was often overlooked.

During my training I grew to love my calling even more. I knew regardless of what I was up against, I would be serving and protecting the streets, my family, friends, and the citizens. As my training came to an end it was time for me to "hit the streets!" As a female recruit, I was warned that I may face disgruntled "old school" male officers and to just take note of it. During my ride-along as a recruit, I was ignored simply because I wasn't a man. I took that experience and used it to shape how I would carry myself with pride, strength, and professionalism. I could not allow my voice to be dismissed or allow myself to continue to get berated. I acknowledged that disparities in representation existed for Latinas, and me joining the department would promote equality. I knew I would have to navigate my way through a male-dominated field.

Being Puerto Rican, co-workers often made assumptions about me—that I grew up in a Latino neighborhood. The truth? I grew up in a neighborhood where we were the only Latino family on the block, for blocks! The stereotypes and internal biases I encountered made me realize the real work wasn't just on the streets, it was within law enforcement itself. Despite moments of disrespect and exclusion, I never wavered. I reset, refocused, and regained control of my purpose. My uniform didn't define me—my integrity, my actions, and my dedication did.

My goal has always been clear: to help change law enforcement interactions with communities and to be a mentor to other female officers. I want to show women officers their presence matters and they don't need to prove themselves to anyone but themselves. I've learned that leadership isn't about titles, it's about inspiring others through action, empathy, and authenticity. The way you treat your fellow peers and those you encounter will follow you throughout your career. Now I've moved into the supervisory role, I want to continue to have a positive impact on other officers.

As a sergeant, my mission is bigger than ever. I want to be the leader I needed when I first started my career. Leadership isn't about rank, it's about responsibility, voice, and service. I want to show women that they belong in every room, they belong in every rank and every decision. I make room at tables for them.

As a sergeant, I try to acknowledge and assist all officers with their accomplishments and needs. I made the rank of sergeant later in my career. Throughout the first sixteen years of my career, there weren't many promotional exams as compared to nowadays. Promotional exams were only given about every eight to ten years. Exams are now given more frequently.

Motherhood reshaped my world. Having twins changed everything, especially when one of them needed medical care. I was fortunate to work in a unit that supported me through it. I wasn't always the most "active" officer by the traditional metrics—arrests, warrants, stops. My worth was not in arrest numbers. It was in every life I impacted; every young lady I inspired to chase her dream. I can honestly say that my numbers were not high due to being inside a unit and that is okay.

As women, especially in this field, we are often expected to work twice as hard to be seen or heard as equal. But I don't chase approval. I know who I am. I work hard, lead by example, and I try to uplift those around me. I work hard to demonstrate my ability to effectively manage, lead, and be an advocate for females in law enforcement. A Latina in law enforcement brings an understanding of the Latin culture, speaks the language, and assists in communities that may be underrepresented. Many officers believe that your numbers or activity label you as the "real police." In reality, your response to a call of service, such as mental health, in progress burglaries, traffic crashes, domestic violence, etc., is doing real police work. The duties and responsibilities of an officer taking calls and monitoring your area helps you understand your community. By responding to calls of service you become more familiar with the citizens and community.

Every encounter with the community and its citizens is an opportunity to rebuild trust and be the police. Understand the oath you took, emerge daily, be proactive and transparent, and engage with a positive mindset. Not all days are positive but take it as a learning opportunity. Continue to grow and exercise your positivity and fill yourself with knowledge, development, communication, empathy, charisma, accountability, and leadership.

This is what leadership looks like. It's not about power. I strive every day to inspire my sisters in blue to rise, grow, and evolve. One goal of mine is to be a positive influence to all officers. Today, as a sergeant, my mission remains clear: to inspire, uplift, and lead with the heart. I want every young woman in this field to know they have the power to lead and encourage them to strive for the best. Lead with a purpose, because that's how we shift the culture of policing. That's how we lead.

During my career as a law enforcement officer, I earned my bachelor's and master's degrees in public safety administration and public safety management while working, raising my children, and holding the line. I even put my doctoral program on pause to study for and pass the sergeant's exam. I chose to fight for that promotion, not just for me, but for every woman who's been told she can't make rank or doesn't belong in rank or simply laughed at. I studied with my children, my husband, and family. My parents raised me to believe that discipline and determination are the keys to success. I worked extra hard to pursue each accomplishment.

I love being an officer and now a sergeant. I love trying to help in any way possible and guiding others' growth throughout their career. I believe my mindset has evolved in this career through personal growth, personal development, and seeking guidance from my mentors who respect, guide, and lead by example. I want to be a role model to young women of all communities and ensure them that they can be a difference. My mentors, both men and women in all ranks, were a grounding force. They appreciate and accept me for who I am. Leadership isn't about always having the answers; it's about showing up, staying humble, and being willing to learn as you go. The fight and passion I have grows daily. A drive to do more, be more—not just for myself, but for my family, my community, and other officers. That is what leaders do. I aspire every day to do this and make it a priority to help others.

A MOMENT OF IMPACT IN LAW ENFORCEMENT

One moment of impact in law enforcement was when I walked across the stage as a sergeant of police. A strong, independent, and confident Latina crossing the stage and making rank was striking. I studied every day for months leading up to the exam. Becoming a sergeant took grit, growth, and guidance. I promised myself to remain humble as I once was an officer. I am thankful my mentors took time to help facilitate this journey into a supervisory role. My mentors contributed with their wisdom, boosted my confidence and held me accountable. They provided encouragement and emotional support. Their influence became part of my leadership DNA. Lead with integrity, heart and courage.

As a sergeant, I now have more of an opportunity to help other female officers. Officers may view me as "tough." It's actually the complete opposite; I understand and identify with them as a female in law enforcement. I see potential and growth, and I want to mentor them for what they may potentially encounter within the department or on the street. Understanding themselves, their standards, and beliefs are critical. I am honest and tell them they will face challenges and hurdles, but to continue to have faith in themselves.

BIOGRAPHY

Nina Rodriguez is an accomplished police sergeant with nineteen years of dedicated service in law enforcement. Throughout her career, she has exhibited unparalleled commitment, resilience, work ethic, and heart. She holds a bachelor's and master's degrees in public safety administration and public safety management, exemplifying her belief in the power of education. Nina's life is a testament to the power of perseverance, education, and family.

She values a well-balanced lifestyle, both physically and mentally. Family plays a central role in Nina's life. She is the proud mother of sixteen-year-old twins, having instilled in them values, morals, principles, and respect guiding them to lead with character and compassion.

Nina is deeply grateful for her family. Her older brother, who serves as her role model and mentor. Her sister-in-law is truly her best friend. The amount of love and appreciation she has for her parents and for their sacrifices, which shaped her upbringing and provided her with the foundation to succeed. She honors the memory of her late mother, the matriarch of the family, who continues to guide her spirit.

She remains a beacon of inspiration for those around her, always encouraging others to pursue their dreams and honor their values.

Nina Rodriguez
rodriguezn5631@gmail.com
IG: @cocochanel454
Facebook: Nina Rodriguez
TikTok: @cocochanel4544

Becoming the Badge

NANCY SANCHEZ

"For my kids, my choices meant stability and hope. They witnessed firsthand what it means to fight for a better life."

For as long as I can remember, I dreamed of becoming a police officer. The first time I put on my uniform, I paused, took a deep breath, and adjusted my badge. In that moment, I didn't just see a reflection in the mirror—I saw every battle I had fought, every tear I had shed, every moment I refused to give up.

That day, I didn't just feel like a police officer—I knew I was meant to be one. Every step I had taken, no matter how painful, had led me here. My journey wasn't just about survival. It was about becoming. And I was becoming exactly who I was meant to be.

Today, when I look in the mirror, I don't just see a police officer. I see a Latina woman who refused to be defined by fear. A woman who walked away from abuse, rebuilt her life and found her place in a profession where her presence alone breaks barriers. A woman who, despite every obstacle, never stopped believing in herself.

But my story isn't just mine. It's the story of every Latina who dares to dream bigger. It's for every woman who's been told no and keeps fighting to prove otherwise. It's for the little girls standing on the sidewalk, whispering, "She looks like me."

My path—a journey of survival, education, and empowerment—is a living testament to strength, resilience, and determination. Today, I serve with integrity, compassion, and unbreakable spirit. Through my work, I don't just protect, I inspire. I remind others that the future is always worth fighting for. My legacy is one of triumph, courage and the unwavering belief that, no matter your past, you have the power to shape your future.

I never imagined that my life's hardships would shape my path into law enforcement. Growing up in Humboldt Park, Chicago, the third oldest of seven sisters, I learned early on the values of responsibility, perseverance, and faith. My parents opened up their own mom-and-pop store, working hard to provide for our family. I was raised in a Catholic household that emphasized dedication, service, and self-reliance.

Like many young girls, I believed in fairy-tale love. I thought I had met my prince charming but that illusion quickly faded as I found myself trapped in a cycle of domestic violence. My ex-husband had a machismo mentality believing that by keeping me pregnant and dependent he could break my spirit and control me. But I had other plans, I was determined to pursue my education and build a better future for myself and my children.

Despite his efforts to hold me back, I pushed forward. I enrolled in college, finished my degree. Every class I took, every assignment I completed was a step toward my independence and empowerment.

It was during this time that I realized I wanted to help others who felt trapped and powerless, just as I once did. I wanted to be a protector, a voice for those who were afraid to speak up. I saw law enforcement as more than just a career; it was a way to serve, to give back, and to make a real difference.

There was a female police officer who responded to one of the most traumatic events of my life, a domestic violence incident that left me broken and afraid. I'll never forget her. She was calm, compassionate, and kind. In that moment, she didn't just protect me, she inspired me that I, too, was meant to be a police officer. Through her empathy and strength, I saw something I didn't know I had in me. The ability to rise, to reclaim control, and to one day be that presence for someone else. That was the moment I knew that law enforcement was my calling. Not because I wanted to be a hero, but because someone once showed up for me when I needed them the most. She helped change the course of my life and now I get to be that person for someone else.

Becoming a police officer has been one of the most fulfilling and rewarding decisions of my life. Over the past six years, I've had the privilege of serving in patrol, community safety teams, and contributing to recruitment efforts, all of which have shaped me both personally and professionally. Each role reinforcing my belief that I am exactly where I am meant to be. As a recruiter, I now help others, especially women and those from diverse backgrounds, so that they, too, have a place in this field. Looking back, my decision to pursue a career in law enforcement was not just a job, it was about reclaiming my power. I chose to stand up, to fight back, and to turn my pain into purpose. Now, every time I put on my uniform, I am reminded of why I started this journey to protect, to inspire, and to be the kind of officer I once needed.

My decision had a profound impact on my children and family. During a period of protest and anti-police views, I wanted my family to know this career was not a mistake. Not all agreed with my career path, but they respected my decision and supported my dream. I wanted my children to see a strong, independent mother who refused to be held back by fear or circumstance.

For my kids, my choices meant stability and hope. They witnessed firsthand what it means to fight for a better life. I wanted them to know that no matter where you come from or what you've endured you always have the power to change your story.

As a Mexican American woman in law enforcement, I was stepping into a male-dominated profession, challenging traditional expectations. My parents were proud but also worried about the dangers I would face. Over time, they saw my passion and purpose and they came to understand that this was more than a job, it was my calling. I feel my family's views have changed. In the end, my decision to pursue a career in law enforcement did not just change my life, it empowered my children, inspired my family, and proved that breaking barriers is not only possible, it's necessary.

Having Latina mentors in law enforcement is crucial. They provide representation, guidance, and support for other Latinas navigating a male-dominated and often culturally challenging field. Their presence helps break down barriers and paves the way for more diversity and equity in policing. Their mentorship influenced how I now mentor others, ensuring the next generation of Latinas in law enforcement feels seen, supported, and empowered.

Representation is more than just a presence. It's a statement. It tells young girls that they belong in spaces where they were once invisible. It tells communities that they have officers who understand them, speak their language, and share their struggles. It tells the world that Latinas are not just here to serve, we are here to lead. But no one breaks barriers alone. Mentorship is the force that turns potential into power. It's the hand that pulls another woman up, the voice that says, "You belong here," even when doubt creeps in.

As a Latina in law enforcement, my experience has been both empowering and eye-opening. From the beginning, I knew I carried more than just a badge I carried my culture, my language and the responsibility of representing women like me in a field where we are still underrepresented. Being a first-generation Mexican American gave me a unique lens through which I see the people I serve, especially in communities that look like the one I grew up in.

One of the biggest lessons I've learned is that being an effective officer isn't just about enforcing the law. It's about connection, compassion, and communication. Speaking Spanish and understanding the culture of the Latino community has often made all the difference. Whether it's calming a panicked mother at the scene of an accident or explaining a legal process to an elderly couple who doesn't speak English, I've learned that trust starts with understanding.

Overtime, I came to understand that being a Latina in this field isn't a limitation, it's an asset. I speak Spanish fluently and that alone has opened doors during countless calls. Being able to communicate with someone in their native language can deescalate tension faster than any tactical strategy. But beyond language, it's the cultural understanding that matters.

To the women who dream of wearing the badge, know that this road will challenge you in ways you never imagined. It won't be easy. You'll see things that stay with you, feel pressures that others may never understand, and carry burdens you can't always share. That's why protecting your mental health is just as important as protecting others. Find balance. Find a hobby that reminds you who you are outside the uniform. Surround yourself with people who lift you up, and never be afraid to ask for help.

I've lost friends, some to the job and some to the weight of it. I've felt the heartbreak of losing someone in the line of duty, and the pain of losing someone to suicide. Those losses changed me. They reminded me that strength also means knowing when to pause, when to breathe, and when to heal. This career can be beautiful and fulfilling, but only if you learn to take care of the woman behind the badge first.

Lessons I've learned along the way have shaped not only my journey, but the way I show up every day in this profession. Push through the doubt. Push through the barriers. Stand firm in your purpose. Support other women, lift each other up, and mentor those who come after you, because we are stronger together. Balance strength with compassion. Lead with heart and never forget the human side of the badge. And always remember your why. You're breaking barriers and making history. Your presence in this field matters more than you know. You are strong, capable, and worthy of this profession. Keep pushing forward. Keep proving them wrong and never stop believing in yourself. We need you. Our communities need you. You are the future of law enforcement. You belong here.

I believe that sharing my story will help others see themselves in this profession. My experience of overcoming domestic abuse gives hope and strength to other survivors. I share my story not to tell you what I've endured, but to remind you of what you're capable of. If I can do it, so can you.

I didn't become a police officer to be a hero. I became one because someone once showed up when I needed them the most. Now, I get to be that person for someone else. That's the real reward.

A MOMENT OF IMPACT IN LAW ENFORCEMENT

One call I'll never forget involved a young woman who had fled her home after years of domestic abuse. She only spoke Spanish and was terrified when we arrived. Her body language was closed off, and she barely looked up. The responding officer tried to ask her questions, but she just nodded, saying "Sí" to everything, clearly not understanding. I stepped in, gently approached her, and started speaking to her in Spanish. I told her, "*Estás segura ahora. Estoy aquí para ayudarte. No estás sola.*" ("You're safe now. I'm here to help you. You're not alone.")

Her eyes filled with tears. She didn't just hear the words; I could see that she felt them. She opened up slowly, telling me about the years of abuse, how she had no family nearby, how she was afraid of losing her children. I listened not just as an officer, but as a woman who had once stood in similar shoes. In that moment I knew that being a Latina—my presence, my culture, my language, and my story—was the reason she felt safe enough to speak. I connected her with the right support, and I followed up with her weeks later. She was starting over, stronger and more hopeful.

That one moment made all the difficult days so worth it. I truly believe that if I hadn't been there, if I hadn't spoken her language or understood the unspoken shame and fear that often surround abuse in our culture, she might have stayed silent. That moment reminded me why I do this work. I'm not just here to protect and serve, I'm here to connect and to show others that there is strength in survival and pride in where we come from.

BIOGRAPHY

Nancy Sanchez is a proud first-generation Mexican American police officer serving the city of Chicago. With six plus years of dedicated service, she has built a reputation as a committed public servant, passionate recruiter, and advocate for diversity in law enforcement.

Born and raised in Chicago's Humboldt Park neighborhood, Nancy grew up in a loving, entrepreneurial household, instilling in her the values of perseverance, dedication, and self-reliance. As the third oldest of seven sisters, she naturally developed a strong sense of responsibility and leadership early in life.

At a young age, Nancy became a mother believing she had found her prince charming. But those dreams quickly turned to hardship as she endured years of domestic violence at the hands of her husband. Refusing to let fear define her, she broke free from the cycle of abuse. In a bold and empowering decision, she also chose to walk away from the successful restaurant business she had built for the sake of her mental and emotional well-being, recognizing that true success isn't just about material achievements; it's about freedom, self-respect, and reclaiming one's future.

With fierce determination, Nancy earned an associate's degree in paralegal studies from Robert Morris College and went on to earn a bachelor's degree in business administration with a concentration in law from Robert Morris University. Emerging strong from a long and painful divorce, she transformed her pain into purpose. With resilience as her foundation, she pursued a career in law enforcement, committed to protecting others and ensuring that no one would ever feel trapped or voiceless in an abusive situation.

Nancy Sanchez
nancysanchez305@yahoo.com

Amor Fati: Embracing All That Shaped Me

THELMA VEGA

"This career has given me purpose, but it's my identity that gives me power."

My father unknowingly inspired me to pursue a career in law enforcement with a simple question: *¿Crees que puedas?—Do you think you could do it?* I took it as a personal challenge. I had always been curious about what it would be like to be a cop—cops always seemed so cool to me. As a little girl, I dreamed of riding a motorcycle and becoming a police officer. I had a very specific department in mind: the Chicago Police Department, the second largest in the nation. Eventually, I got to do both.

My father's question stayed with me. It became the quiet engine behind everything I've strived for. My dad lit the fire in me to prove what I could do. In many ways, my decision to join the Chicago Police Department—and the assignments I've taken on—deeply impacted my parents. They spent countless sleepless nights worrying about my safety. My family often rearranged holidays around my schedule so I wouldn't miss out. Just as their sacrifices shaped me, I know my path has shaped them, too.

To understand my purpose, choices, and drive, it's essential to know where I come from—my roots, my people, my foundation. I'm the middle daughter of three, born to Mexican immigrants from humble beginnings. My mother's story is one of resilience and unimaginable hardship. The second oldest of eight children, she began working on farms at the age of nine to help support her family. She endured a level of poverty no child should experience—yet in her town, during those times, it was common. She once told me about the day her younger brother lay in her arms, weak and fading. He died that night. She didn't know then—it was from malnutrition, a harsh reality where she grew up.

Driven by curiosity and a desire for something more, my mother made her way alone to the United States. When she arrived, she met my father—her neighbor, also from the same small town.

My dad was everything—smart, funny, wise, cultured, and kind. But he carried the weight of a difficult upbringing, and it left him shy and self-conscious. His gentle, timid soul struggled to recover from life's blows. He didn't recognize what I see so clearly now, even more so since he's no longer here: he had boundless potential. He could have set the world on fire.

Now that I understand that, I carry his unrealized potential with me. His spirit lives on in my sisters and me. This is my fuel, my drive. I won't take opportunities for granted. I'll use them to rise—and to honor my parents' sacrifices. My father's legacy lives through me. I will make them proud. I know he's with me—I still hear him say, *"Todo va estar bien."* Everything is going to be alright. And I know that it is.

My sisters have shared both the weight and the beauty of this journey. They've adjusted plans, celebrated my milestones, and stood by me in every season. Even when I doubted myself, they reminded me who I am. God knew what He was doing when He made us sisters.

When I think about the strength that's carried me through this journey, I know it didn't start with me—it started with them. From my mother, I learned resilience and bravery—the will to push through no matter what, and the unshakable truth that her strength lives in me. Strength born of sacrifice, rooted in love, shaped by hard work, and carried with quiet grace. I come from courageous women who endure—and because of that, I rise. From my father, I learned vision and belief—sparked by a simple question that grew into confidence. His words stayed with me, shaping how I saw myself and who I believed I could become. He pushed me to recognize my potential and helped me believe in a version of myself I hadn't yet imagined. From my sisters, I learned loyalty and love—the kind that shows up without being asked and stays through every storm. They've been my mirrors, my anchors, and my greatest champions. Because of them, I never walk alone. This career has given me purpose—but it's my identity that gives me power. My strength doesn't just come from what I've trained for—it comes from where I come from, who I carry with me, and the legacy I carry forward.

Upon being accepted and entering the police academy I didn't know what to expect. Six months of training introduced me to a new culture, new discipline, and new challenges. I loved the physical training but feared the firearms portion—I'd never held a gun. Failing meant losing everything, but with practice came confidence.

After graduating from the academy, I was assigned to patrol in a South Side district and eventually joined the district's tactical team. At the time, we had a handful of female officers—something not common in many districts.

While working a temporary assignment in another district, my partner and I walked into a room full of male officers. Noticing the absence of women, my partner mentioned that our team had several female officers. A male supervisor quickly responded, "Yeah, we don't have that problem here"—referring to the presence of women on tactical teams—as I stood right beside him.

Without missing a beat, my partner pushed back: "Actually, the women on our team are more proactive than a lot of the guys—real go-getters." Hearing him say that meant everything.

Moments like that are reminders of the subtle and not-so-subtle challenges women have faced and, in some cases, still face in this profession. While we've come a long way, there's still work to be done. Those moments deepened my awareness and showed me the power of allies who speak up when it matters most.

Seeking a challenge and wanting to grow, I applied and was selected to join the Fugitive Apprehension Unit, part of a federal task force. That assignment remains my favorite to this day. We worked in teams of about ten but operated in pairs. I was partnered with another female officer—someone I didn't know at the time but would soon come to deeply respect. Though we didn't choose each other, we quickly became a strong team.

Our mission was clear: safely apprehend fugitives wanted for violent crimes like murder and sexual assault. We were often underestimated because of our gender and size—but that worked in our favor. We used it strategically, relying on observation, communication, and finesse. There were times we were able to talk targets into cuffs without force. There were other times when we had to rely on our training, tactics, and teammates to safely make the arrest. We were prepared for both.

Sitting on surveillance, watching a target emerge, moving in and making the arrest, then calling the victim or their family to say, "We got them"—those moments never left me. The emotion in their voices reminded me of the importance of what we were doing.

Our strength came from teamwork and trust. We did our homework, we planned meticulously, and we supported one another. I always tell young officers, learn how to talk to people. Size and strength only go so far—connection, communication, and compassion are what truly get the job done.

One of our first conversations as partners was about the future. She asked what I wanted to do in this career. I hadn't thought beyond getting to that unit, but I told her I wanted to be a detective. She said her goal was to become a sergeant and move up the chain. Ironically, the opposite ended up happening. At the time, I couldn't picture myself as a sergeant—Latina supervisors were rare, and the department hadn't offered a promotional exam in nearly a decade.

When the department finally announced a Sergeant Promotional Exam. I didn't know how I'd do, but I didn't want to miss the opportunity. I shot my shot and I was ultimately promoted to sergeant a few years later.

Becoming a sergeant requires a major shift in mindset. As an officer, your focus is on completing the mission; as a sergeant, it's about leading, guiding, and being responsible for those carrying it out. That transition took some time. As a sergeant, I developed my leadership style by learning from both the supervisors I admired and those I never wanted to emulate. I remembered what it felt like to be overlooked—standing at a scene while questions were directed only to my male partner, even when I had led the case. In those moments, I felt invisible. I made a promise to myself: no one I worked with would ever feel that way.

Not all challenges came from where I expected. As a sergeant, I was taking attendance during roll call when a female officer responded with "princess"—instead of using my rank or "ma'am," as is customary. Meant as a joke, it undercut me—and it stung. I had spent years proving I belonged. I didn't expect it from someone who looked like me. I addressed it privately, and she sincerely apologized. That moment reminded me: real leadership lifts others—even when they don't lift you.

Shortly after the lieutenant's exam was announced, my father was diagnosed with stage four cancer. We studied together, talking through scenarios over the phone. This time, he didn't ask if I could do it—he told me I could. I was promoted and soon appointed acting commander of a citywide unit. I knew how that might be perceived, so I leaned on my mentors. One reminded me that my career had prepared me for this—that presence, authenticity, and connection are what truly define leadership.

That role taught me that leadership isn't always loud—sometimes, the greatest impact comes simply from showing up. Leading a citywide unit gave me the opportunity to shape culture, prioritize officer wellness, and be more intentional about how we supported one another—not just operationally but as people. It also allowed me to show up in ways that made others feel seen and valued.

One moment that stays with me happened on a cold day when I checked on two tactical officers guarding a crime scene. I didn't know them personally; I just wanted to make sure they were okay. As I approached, I was met with warm smiles. They were Latina partners—something I rarely saw when I was coming up. They shared how proud they were to see a Latina lieutenant, and I echoed their sentiment. I encouraged them to keep going, to keep growing. It was a brief exchange, but it reminded me why presence matters. Sometimes, just seeing someone who looks like you in leadership can make the impossible feel possible. That moment still encourages me. I was proud of them and of how far we've come as a department. I hope I encouraged them as much as they inspired me.

Not long after, I hit a breaking point. I was exhausted—trying to be present for my unit, my department, and most of all, for my dad. Around that time, an officer was killed in the line of duty. The loss hit hard—several on my team had a personal connection to him. We were all carrying a lot and holding each other up the best we could.

Then came the moment that still feels surreal: our family was called into the doctor's office and told it was time to stop treatment and begin palliative care. In shock, I hugged my father, wept, and apologized. He comforted me, saying, "Todo va estar bien." He told me he had lived—and that was enough.

Grief came in waves. In his final days, we sat together watching music documentaries, building playlists, and talking about everything but death. The last time I saw him, something shifted—and I felt it the moment I left. At a stoplight, something told me to turn around. I believe God gave me the chance to say goodbye. I held his hand, told him how proud I was of him, and thanked him for the life he lived and the impact he had on mine. When we asked for advice, he told us not to take life too seriously. We told each other we loved one another, and I promised to return the next day.

His passing forced me to pause. I stepped away and traveled to Isla Holbox, a small island in Mexico, where I found peace in the nature he once dreamed of seeing. It's taken time to release the guilt of not doing more, not being there more. But I'm learning to give myself grace. As my sister reminds me—we did what we could. And that was enough.

Over the years, I've connected with people from all walks of life. That diversity of perspective has made me a better cop, a better leader, and a better person. Connection is vital—but too often, we forget that as we climb the ranks and chase the next goal.

I've also faced moments of doubt, grief, and transition—times that tested me both personally and professionally. In those seasons, I leaned heavily on the wisdom and presence of others. My family's unwavering support has been the foundation of everything I do. Their belief in me, their love, and their constant encouragement have carried me through every chapter of this journey.

Along the way, I've been guided by mentors—some expected, others who appeared just when I needed them most. Their insight helped me navigate challenges, reminded me to lead with empathy and presence, and showed me that growth doesn't happen alone. It was my mentors who taught me that leadership doesn't come from a rank—it comes from humility. And it's that humility that allows us to connect, to lead with purpose, and to leave something better behind.

Among those guides was a voice I'd long admired—Sandra Cisneros. A chance meeting with my favorite author turned into a moment of unexpected clarity. Her words gave me the courage to share my story—one that had been forming quietly for years. Her generosity and encouragement remain a gift I carry with me.

Now, my goal is to pay it forward—to support and guide the next generation, just as others have done for me.

A MOMENT OF IMPACT IN LAW ENFORCEMENT

Early in my career, I lost a classmate from the academy—a good friend—who was killed in the line of duty while investigating shots fired on the South Side of Chicago. Alex was a year younger than me, full of potential, drive, and positivity. His death—my first experience losing someone my age, in uniform, and a close friend—shook me to my core.

Alex often crosses my mind when I don my uniform. I wonder what life would've been like for him. I have no doubt he would have continued to excel and leave a lasting mark on the department. That tragedy became a turning point. It inspired me to live fully—to seize every opportunity, to just go for it.

While considering how to spend my furlough, I reflected on his sacrifice and remembered sound advice from a veteran officer: "You can always make more money, but you can't make more time." I chose to embrace that wisdom.

Since then, travel has broadened my perspective and deepened my gratitude—not just for the world, but for my journey. On one trip, I met the first Saudi woman to be licensed by her government as a pilot. I had always seen myself as just a cop, but she made me realize the honor and privilege of serving as a Latina in law enforcement.

Experiences like that are a powerful form of education. They've reshaped how I view service, leadership, and authenticity on this job.

BIOGRAPHY

Thelma Vega joined the Chicago Police Department in December 2005 and has dedicated nearly twenty years to public service. She was promoted to sergeant in March 2017 and lieutenant in August 2022. Throughout her career, she has served in various roles, including in the Patrol Division, the US Marshals Great Lakes Fugitive Task Force, the Communications and News Affairs Division, and the City-Wide Community Safety Team.

A first-generation Mexican American, Thelma's family hails from Guanajuato, Mexico. She grew up in Summit, Illinois, and is a graduate of Argo Community High School. She earned a bachelor's degree in political science and sociology from Northern Illinois University. She is a graduate of the National FBI Academy and the DC Police Leadership Academy at the Metropolitan Police Department in Washington, DC. Additionally, she holds a graduate certificate in criminal justice education from the University of Virginia, where she is currently pursuing a master of public safety.

In 2022, Thelma earned a Chicago/Midwest Emmy nomination as an executive producer for a short film about a fallen officer. She is also a proud member of the Chicago Latina Foundation, an organization committed to empowering Latinas through advocacy, community, leadership, education, and mentorship.

Outside of law enforcement, she is an avid traveler who has visited over twenty-five countries and has a deep appreciation for music and the arts.

Thelma Vega
LinkedIn: Thelma Vega

ABOUT THE AUTHOR

Michelle J. Velasquez is a proud wife to Martin Arteaga and mother of four—Marty, Izan, Joe, and Adaleah. She recently transitioned out of government service after a distinguished sixteen-year career with US Customs and Border Protection, where she held key roles on the Currency and Border Security Team, in Airport Operations, and as a liaison with HSI Narcotics and the DHS Fusion Center. She also mentored youth through the CBP Explorers program, supported workforce development, and championed inclusion as chair of the Diversity, Equity, and Inclusion Committee.

As an academy instructor, Michelle helped shape the future of federal law enforcement and holds a Traumas of Law Enforcement certification from Concerns of Police Survivors (COPS). Her service earned numerous honors, including the Commissioner's Unit Citation, US Interdiction Coordinator Award, Chicago Police Joint Operations Award, CBP Advisor of the Year, and the Federal Executive Board's Intergovernmental Outstanding Law Enforcement Team Award.

Now focused on financial empowerment, Michelle is the founder of Virtuous Wealth Building, a certified financial master coach trainer, author, speaker, and facilitator with the Worklife Training Institute. She holds her master's degree from Loyola University Chicago and has completed multiple leadership, financial, real estate, and entrepreneurial training programs.

Michelle became a co-author with Latinas in Finance, marking the start of her writing journey. She went on to publish *Spending for Chiquis' Birthday Surprise, 9 Steps to Achieve a Millionaire Mindset,* and *Clarity is Power: Know Your Numbers, Own Your Power.* Alongside her writing, Michelle is an active real estate investor, committed to diversifying her income and helping others do the same.

Fueled by her belief in lifelong learning and the power of education, Michelle remains dedicated to empowering Latina women to dream boldly, pursue financial freedom, and create legacies of abundance—for themselves and their communities.

Michelle J. Velasquez
Financial Coach | Speaker | Author
info@vwbcoaching.com
www.vwbcoaching.com
LinkedIn: Michelle J. Velasquez
Michelle@LatinasinLawEnforcement.com

ABOUT THE AUTHOR

Esmeralda Samaniego has dedicated twenty-two years to federal law enforcement, proudly serving on the front lines to protect the nation's borders, enforce laws, and prevent threats. Her role demanded vigilance, service to country, and unwavering integrity.

Now serving as a program manager in the Chicago Field Office, she oversees initiatives that support officer well-being and strengthen community engagement. She also serves as the Chicago Field Office Honor Guard commander, a national recruiter, a chaplain on the Resiliency Team, and head advisor of the Explorer Program—mentoring the next generation of law enforcement leaders.

A proud Latina raised in a faith-based home, she honors the sacrifices of her parents and siblings by breaking barriers and striving to shine in everything she does. Whether in uniform or on any day, she carries their strength with her—always going above and beyond to make them proud.

Known as "Wonder Woman" for her extraordinary multi-tasking, she has balanced a demanding federal law enforcement career, serves as a caregiver to both parents with the help of her siblings, competed professionally in bodybuilding for eight years, completed five marathons to date, and danced on major bachata and salsa stages.

She is the recipient of many prestigious awards with the US Customs and Border Protection, including Advisor of the Year, Federal Employee of the Year, Federal Executive Board Outstanding Law Enforcement Team Award, Federal Executive Board Citizens Services Team Award, and the Annual Commissioner's Award. Yet her greatest accomplishment remains the legacy she continues to build through service and mentorship.

Esmeralda Samaniego
Officer | Mentor | Author
Esmeralda@LatinasinLawEnforcement.com

www.ingramcontent.com/pod-product-compliance
Lightning Source LLC
Chambersburg PA
CBHW070042100426
42740CB00013B/2772